ECONOMIC GROWTH
AND DECLINING SOCIAL WELFARE

ECONOMIC GROWTH

AND
DECLINING

SOCIAL WELFARE

XENOPHON ZOLOTAS

NEW YORK UNIVERSITY PRESS

NEW YORK and LONDON

1981

Printed in Athens, Greece
at the Bank of Greece Printing Works

"Εἰ βούλει πλούσιον Πυθοκλέα ποιῆσαι, μή χρημάτων προστίθει, τῆς δέ ἐπιθυμίας ἀφαίρει".

"If you wish to make Pythocles rich, do not give him more money, but diminish his desire".

(Epicurus to Idomeneus. Stobaeus, Floril. XVII 24)

PROLOGUE

It was in the early sixties that I first became concerned with the main line of argument developed in the present essay, namely the divergence between the rate of economic growth and the level of affluence on the one hand and the rate of increase in social welfare on the other. At that time, the undesirable effects of affluence were not as acute as they are today, nor had they aroused the interest of scientific circles to the extent they have lately.

Until well into the seventies the concurrence of various commitments and adverse circumstances prevented me from making any significant progress in my research effort, albeit, at times, I was able to give serious thought to some specific aspects of the subject. Over the past five years, however, I have managed to devote a good deal of my free time to an analysis of the effects of economic growth on social welfare. In this respect, what has impressed me has been the continuous discrepancy between the rate of economic growth and increments in social welfare in advanced industrial societies.

As I see it, the problem is what type of further economic growth would be "optimal", i.e. conducive to the maximisation of overall social welfare. This question, of course, is not applicable to developing countries, whose daily experiences are extreme scarcities and privations; it applies solely to affluent societies, where unqualified economic growth has led not only to a faster depletion of natural resources, but also to a rapidly deteriorating physical environment, to the estrangement of human beings and to soaring social costs.

I have tried to present as accurate and objective calculations as possible and to reach valid results as far as relations between economic growth and well-being are concerned. This, of course, does not preclude that some estimates might be below or above the mark, since some components of social cost or benefit do not always lend themselves to quantification and precise measurement. Although such inaccuracies might be detected, I believe that their presence will not alter the general conclusions of this study.

During the writing of this essay I had the benefit of valuable assistance from Mrs. Anna Alexopoulos, to whom I extend my sincere thanks. I would like to express my appreciation to Professors William Baumol, Robert Grosse, Robert Hawkins, Edmond Malinvaud and James Tobin for kindly undertaking to read the manuscript and make constructive comments. I would also like to thank my Greek colleagues, Professors George Crimbas and Demetrius Plessas, for their remarks on the text.

It would be an omission if I failed to express my thanks to Mr. D. Papanastassiou and Mr. N. Alexopoulos, who assisted in the computations, and to Mr. M. Nicolinakos, who has taken care of the editing.

August 1981   XENOPHON ZOLOTAS

CONTENTS

Prologue   *ix*

Introduction   1

Chapter One: Capital Accumulation in Different
Phases of Economic Development   5
I.   Historical Background   5
II. Some Negative Effects of Economic Growth   8
III. The Scope of the Present Essay   14
     Appendix to Chapter One   21
     Notes to Introduction and Chapter One   25

Chapter Two: The Total Social Welfare Function   31
     Notes to Chapter Two   38

Chapter Three: Index of the Economic Aspects of
Welfare   43
I.   Introductory Remarks   43
II. Theoretical and Empirical Compilation of
     the EAW-Index   44
     1. Items Deducted from Private Consumption
        for a Closer Approximation to the EAW-Index   47
        (a) Durable consumer goods   47
        (b) Advertising   47
        (c) Natural resources   49
        (d) Rapid growth and the rising
            social cost of environmental pollution   60
            Air Pollution   65
            Water Pollution   68
            Solid Waste Disposal   69
        (e) The cost of commuting   72
        (f) Private health and education outlays of
            an investment or corrective nature   79

2. Items Added to Private Consumption in
the Construction of the EAW-Index   86
   (a) Services from the stock of public capital   86
   (b) Services from durable consumer goods   87
   (c) Household services   90
   (d) Leisure time   92
   (e) Public sector services, relating mainly
      to expenditure on education and health   98
III. Summary of Empirical Findings   101
    Notes to Chapter Three   112

Chapter Four: Quality of Life Indicators   131
I.   General Remarks   131
II.   Subjective Indicators   136
III. Objective Indicators   144
   1. Crime   146
   2. Physical Health   155
   3. Mental Health   158
IV. General Conclusions   161
    Notes to Chapter Four   164

Epilogue   177
    Notes to Epilogue   189

Index of Names   193

TABLES

1. Gross National Product and Private Consumption   45
2. Private Expenditure on Durable Consumer Goods   47
3. Advertising Expenditure   48
4. Expenditure on Specific Basic Raw Materials   59
5. Control Cost for Air Pollution   66
6. Total Damages 1970   67
7. Damage Cost Due to Air Pollution   67
8. Control Cost for Water Pollution   69

9. Control Cost for Solid Waste Disposal 70
10. Cost Due to Environmental Pollution 71
11. Ways of Commuting to and from Place of Work 75
12. Cost of Commuting to and from Place of Work 77
13. Private Expenditure on Health 81
14. Private Expenditure on Education 84
15. Imputed Value of Services of Public Buildings that Contribute to an Increase in Economic Welfare 87
16. Imputed Value of Services from Consumer Durables 89
17. Imputed Value of Household Services 92
18. Imputed Value of Leisure Time 97
19. Public Consumption 99
20. Magnitudes Forming the EAW-Index 104
21. The EAW-Index and its Ratio to GNP 106
22. Economic Welfare Elasticity with Respect to GNP 108
23. GNP and Items Included in the EAW-Index 110
24. Items to Be Deducted from or Added to Private Consumption, as a Percentage of GNP 111
25. Homicide Victims per 100,000 Population 147
26. Violent Crimes per 100,000 Population 148
27. Divorces per 1,000 Population 150

CHARTS

1. Total social welfare as a function of Gross National Product 16
2. GNP and private consumption through time 46
3. Items deducted from private consumption (consumer durables, cost of pollution, commuting cost, cost of resource depletion) 78
4. Items deducted from private consumption (health, advertising, education) 85
5. Items added to private consumption (value of leisure time and of household services) 100

6. Items added to private consumption (services of consumer durables, public consumption, services of public buildings)   100
7. Economic aspects of social welfare versus GNP, at 1972 prices   108
8. Indices of GNP and economic aspects of welfare (includes cost of resource depletion)   109
9. Indices of GNP and economic aspects of welfare   109
10. Homicide victims   149
11. Violent crimes   149
12. Divorces   151

INTRODUCTION

Between the end of the Second World War and the early seventies, the unrestrained pursuit of further economic growth became a typical syndrome of affluent societies.[1] This "growth-mania" was fostered by a sense of euphoria induced by new and often energy-intensive technologies. The very low cost of liquid fuels until 1973 and rapid technological innovation were the corner-stones of economic progress, the pace and duration of which were historically unique. However, accelerated economic growth has caused grave damages to the ecosystem, a fast depletion of non-renewable natural resources and a general decline in the quality of life.

The central theme of this essay concerns the problems associated with economic growth and focuses on the following queries: has continuing growth in the mature industrial economies brought about a commensurate improvement in social welfare? Has increased material well-being been accompanied by a better quality of life, greater personal happiness and greater social peace together with the conservation of the ecosystem?

This research is an attempt to show that, beyond a certain point, economic growth may cease to promote social welfare. In fact, it would appear that, when an industrial society reaches an advanced stage of affluence, the rate of increase in social welfare drops below the rate of economic growth and tends ultimately to become negative.

Here, however, another query is in order: given the present wasteful pattern of economic growth in affluent societies, has it at least been possible to narrow the gap between poor and rich nations? Once again, the question does not admit of an affirmative answer. Despite unprecedented rates of economic growth throughout the post-war period, the industrial nations have been slow in assisting the 800 million people of the undernourished nations of the Third World out of their poverty. On generally accepted evidence, the gap between rich and poor countries has actually widened.[2,3]

As was mentioned above, a powerful impetus to economic growth after the Second World War was given by technological innovation.[4] Modern technology is by nature energy-consuming, capital and material intensive, and even "environment intensive" in the sense that it contributes to the deterioration of the environment.[5] One of the reasons may be that modern industrial technology is to a considerable extent a result of the spin-off effects of military technology, detached from social needs and developed primarily for purposes other than those contributing to society's progress. Furthermore, the increasing degree of specialisation and division of labour has had a "sterilising" effect; it eventually led to the estrangement of the working individual from a coherent view of the production process. Thus, man has become an appendage and a servant of that process and not its master.

Another reason for the rapid advances in this type of technology is that energy could be obtained at artificially low cost, at least until the early seventies. The availability of relatively cheap and plentiful energy also explains the wasteful nature of many of the processes embodying high technology. There is often the impression that these have afforded a better standard of living for society, while in fact they have contributed to the increase in waste.

The problems attributed to modern technology are aggravated by a vicious circle which seems to link technical change to the process of economic growth in advanced industrial societies. Although technology has undoubtedly played a prominent role in raising productivity, which in turn has been a driving force behind rapid economic expansion, the production-consumption cycle is constantly generating new wants. The satisfaction of these new wants requires the development of yet newer technologies, which result in the dynamic extension of the technological frontier existing at any given point of time.

Although the side-effects of a specific technological mix last as long as the latter remains unchanged, it is quite likely that technological breakthroughs will eventually solve most of the existing problems.[6] Meanwhile, however, in the absence of major achievements in producing and economising on energy, in pollution control etc., mankind will have to go through a rather lengthy period of readjustment. The first signs of the crisis are already apparent.

One clear implication of this analysis is that the development policies of rich nations have often been unwise and self-defeating, to such an extent that they may be likened to a contemporary "Jar of the Danaides"; such policies have neither improved social welfare in affluent communities nor helped the poor nations of the world out of poverty and famine.

Considerable theoretical and empirical research has been undertaken in recent years, on particular aspects of the economics of welfare. This essay attempts to document a global approach to the question of social welfare, so as to include not only the economic aspects but also those factors that determine the quality-of-life aspect. The discussion focuses on the conditions under which social welfare in the rich industrial nations may be increasing at an ever diminishing rate or may eventually show an absolute decline as a consequence of the unqualified pursuit of economic expansion.

It should be emphasised that this essay refers to industrialised countries which, in the process of furthering economic growth to the point of affluence, have overlooked the possible hazardous effects of growth on social well-being. The purpose of the present study is to confirm that what has to be maximised is not economic growth *per se,* but overall social welfare. This can only be achieved by "optimising" the path and content of economic growth. Thus, what this study stands for is more of a better life.

CHAPTER ONE

CAPITAL ACCUMULATION IN DIFFERENT PHASES OF ECONOMIC DEVELOPMENT

I. HISTORICAL BACKGROUND

The principal concept underlying the free market system — *la civilisation de toujours plus* — is the need for perpetual economic growth.[7] Attainment of this goal provides the legitimation basis of the free market economy.[8,9]

There is nothing novel in this concept. In the last quarter of the 18th century, Adam Smith wrote: "It deserves to be remarked that it is in the progressive state... that the condition of the labouring poor... seems to be the happiest and the most comfortable. It is hard in the stationary, and miserable in the declining state. The progressive state is in reality the cheerful and the hearty state to all the different orders of the society. The stationary is dull; the declining melancholy."[10]

The foregoing statement is of fundamental significance, because it sums up the *raison d'être* of the industrial system and the root causes of its legitimation crisis should economic growth no longer be feasible.

It could therefore be said that Adam Smith formulated, implicitly but cogently, the principle that continuous accumulation of wealth is the quintessence of advanced industrialism, its supreme driving force, and the necessary condition for its smooth and proper functioning. Here it must be stated that in most advanced socialist countries too, capital accumulation, in the process of their industrialisation, has created, *mutatis mutandis*, analogous problems.[11]

The pro-growth philosophy that dominated economic thought for nearly two centuries has recently come under serious scrutiny and attack not only by the advocates of economic systems opposed to that of individualist organisation but by the very proponents of the free market economy. Nevertheless, this philosophy should be viewed in the actual historical context prevailing at any point of time. Thus, the classical concept of the need for constantly growing material wealth was embodied in the New Frontier ideology at a time when rapid growth either did not have the visibly negative impact it has today, or its unfavourable effects were relatively insignificant, compared to the social benefits obtained.

The classical economists, however, had predicted with deep concern that economic growth would cease altogether. This would happen in the long run owing to population growth and the law of diminishing returns on land, and would undoubtedly be followed by adverse repercussions on the economic aspects of social welfare.[12] It was only J. S. Mill who held a diametrically opposed view. Although he also foresaw the eventual inevitability of the stationary state, he was optimistic about the future. Exercising amazing foresight, J. S. Mill predicted the problems that have arisen more than one hundred years after his death.[13] It may therefore be said that he was the precursor of those who in our times question the need for continuous economic growth. For it is a fact that, over the last ten or twenty years, economic growth in the industrial countries has been looked upon with increasing scepticism regarding its ultimate effect on total social welfare.[14]

The positive view of economic growth taken by classical economists was historically understandable during the stage of primary accumulation, since it was only through successive increases in the national product that it would be possible to rid the population of the then almost universal state of poverty. In subsequent stages of economic growth, however, this view lost much of its relevance. When a society has secured for the majority of its members the satisfaction of their basic needs and has reached or is approaching the stage of affluence, different options and processes emerge. The mere continuation of the accumulation process in the new setting tends to make a radical change in the one-to-one correspondence that existed in previous stages between economic growth and social well-being. Of course, such changes do not take place overnight; they occur gradually and keep pace with social progress and the level and structure of economic activity.

Moreover, successive stages of economic growth reflect a variety of socio-economic institutions, alterations in interpersonal relationships, and even serious changes in the physical environment itself. These dynamically changing processes were definitely seeded in the very early stages of social organisation. They acquire real importance, however, in the advanced stages of economic growth, when the one-to-one correspondence between growth and social well-being tends to break down.

In contemporary affluent societies, the lack of balance between cultural and moral values on the one hand and technological achievements on the other — the latter being mostly aimed at improving the material aspects of human life — represents a virtual "hubris" against the universal natural laws that are disregarded in the process of economic growth. This "hubris", a result of the reckless pursuit of economic growth, underlies the entire spectrum of crises faced by mankind at present.

In the past, the contingency of capital accumulation slowing down or even coming to a complete standstill was attributed by political economists to such tendencies as population growth and diminishing returns on land. In the last two decades, however, this latent state of stagnation has begun to be viewed as the outcome of hitherto neglected factors, such as environmental pollution, the depletion of natural resources, the energy problem, etc. These unfavourable developments could only be averted or moderated by a new major technological breakthrough. Until then, however, the problem of distribution will remain particularly acute, though not only as increasingly pressing demand for a more equitable distribution of income and wealth but also as a claim to a generally fairer life, in the sense that every human being has an inalienable right to an equal share in the opportunities of a decent life.

II. SOME NEGATIVE EFFECTS OF ECONOMIC GROWTH

The specific problems facing mature industrial economies —namely those that are approaching or have reached a state of affluence—appear to be of quite recent origin and are linked to the historically unique rates of economic growth attained in these economies after the Second World War. There are two interrelated reasons for the ever wider divergence between the rate of economic growth and the pace at which the level of social welfare is rising in today's affluent societies. One is induced "consumerism";[15] the other is the broad spectrum of demonstrably negative effects of growth on social welfare.

Consumerism is examined in connection with the creation and satisfaction of human wants in contemporary industrial societies. Accordingly, human wants are broadly classified into inherent or absolute and socially conditioned or relative.[16] Those in the former category can be satisfied fairly easily; by his very nature, man needs food, clothing and shelter. The needs of someone leading a secluded life and not exposed to modern living conditions are extremely few, while the wants of a modern city-dweller seem to be almost insatiable. This is due to the fact that human preferences are subject to constant change and expansion; they are learned by or imposed upon individual consumers in a dynamic process of advertising and emulation.

As inherent wants exist irrespective of the operation of the socio-economic system, economic progress tends to satisfy the greatest part of them. Once they are satisfied, continuous growth extends society's effective range of opportunities and leads to an enhancement of social welfare.

By contrast, since a large part of relative wants are the product of persuasive salesmanship, they are among the symptoms of modern consumerism. As the following analysis shows, the satisfaction of a good many relative wants is not necessarily conducive to an increase in social welfare, for there exists a positive feedback effect between them and the process of economic growth. This means that, parallel to the production of new goods, economic growth constantly creates new wants, thereby predetermining which goods must be produced to satisfy them. These are not the normal kind of social wants reflecting the essential change and variety that differentiate human beings from biologically inferior forms of life. Quite the contrary, these are wants related to the constant quest for social status that characterises affluent societies, and they change at a tremendous rate. Obviously, the dividing line between the normal penchant for variety and change on the one hand and today's rapidly increasing needs on the other is hard to draw. All the same, the limit must surely lie at the point where social wants begin to change at an accelerating pace. At the same time, their satisfaction aggravates the feelings of anxiety and insecurity, instead of being a source of pleasure and greater welfare, since new wants are always far more pressing than those already satisfied.

In the framework of modern economies, the normal process of creating and satisfying human wants has led to a distorted pattern of behaviour. Thus, economic growth appears as the necessary means to match new, ever increasing "fancy wants" with the anxiety inherent in trying to satisfy them. What characterises affluent societies, besides the attainment of uniquely high rates of economic growth, is the "revolution of expectations" which is interwoven with the endless creation of new wants that can only be satisfied by ever larger amounts of material wealth. After man had met his basic needs for food, clothing, shelter and recreation, he became a modern Sisyphus, condemned forever to chase the elusive mirage of happiness through the fulfilment of continuously rising wants. The result is that today's consumer is always in a state of "instant" equilibrium. The gap between his wants and their satisfaction remains and is even widening, while the frustration caused by failure to satisfy fabricated wants offsets the pleasure gained from those wants that have already been satisfied.

One salient feature of today's economic life is not the enjoyment offered by the use of modern achievements, but the everlasting effort to obtain more and more novel goods. For the level of aspirations, both of individuals and of society as a whole, undergoes continuous parallel shifts that keep the gap between material output and social welfare unbridged. It is therefore doubtful whether an increase in the material product — as realised in today's mature industrial economies — extends the effective range of opportunities or is simply illusory. Actually, such increases in the material product merely raise the social cost of production, while keeping the level of social welfare unchanged or even lowering it.

Of course, these remarks can only stand when overconsumption becomes a goal in itself by turning into a pathological symptom of insatiable affluence. No one is liable to overlook, however, the merits of a system that can ensure a sufficient supply of durable and other goods to liberate man from need and toil, provided that this process does not generate stress and anxiety instead of relief and contentment.

There are numerous examples of economic activity in support of the previous argument; for instance, the fashion industry, through the subjective obsolescence of existing products, is actually a constant source of stress and dissatisfaction. Similarly, consumer durables very often fail to improve social welfare owing to their complexity and the artificial obsolescence to which they are subject.[17] Another class of products is that of "defensive" or corrective goods, including pharmaceuticals. It is, in fact, impossible to argue that overconsumption of drugs, for instance, enhances social welfare. To a considerable extent, excessive use of such preparations could be regarded as part of an overall effort to combat the negative effects of stressful living. Yet, a proliferation of fabricated wants is observed even in the pharmaceutical industry, so that the world market is virtually flooded with tens of thousands of proprietary medicines, rather than the few hundreds actually considered necessary by the World Health Organisation.

The vastness and complexity of the market deprive the consumer of the perfect knowledge he is presumed to possess. In the meantime, while advertising is supposed to come and facilitate his choice, today it often has the opposite effect of further obscuring whatever knowledge of the market the consumer may have. It should be stressed that subjective obsolescence of goods, which reduces the consumer's ultimate satisfaction, is observed when, for instance, fashion and advertising overstep their normally expected roles. On the other hand, if informative advertising, as opposed to suggestive or persuasive, operated rationally and within acceptable limits, it would help the consumer to get to know constantly more of the alternatives offered in an imperfect market. It would thus create information pools without which precise knowledge would be practically inaccessible to the individual consumer. Similarly, fashion would afford the opportunity for variety and change, which are primary requirements for a successful social life. Affluent societies, however, seem to have passed the point beyond which the satisfaction offered by the operation of such mechanisms turns into discontent.

The preceding arguments are centred on consumerism as a factor serving to distort the positive relationship existing between economic growth and social welfare. Needless to say, the syndrome implied by the term "consumerism" is largely psychological, and it does not cover the totality of causes underlying the change in the above mentioned relationship.

There is a broad spectrum of objective and quantifiable factors, ranging from the wasteful use of natural resources to the loss of time and life due to traffic congestion in major urban centres or to the huge social cost of environmental pollution. Such factors suggest that the actual cost of economic growth is too high to be offset by any positive effects it may have on social welfare. In the production process, purely decentralised methods of resource allocation unchecked by corrective levies or lump-sum taxes and subsidies prevent the "internalisation" of very important external diseconomies in the production function. If such negative factors are persistently neglected, the equilibrium of the ecosystem will be disturbed while social costs will rise steeply as a direct consequence.

Most of the factors which remain external to the production process are complex magnitudes. To take one example, the cost of urbanisation includes the increasing amounts of time and money spent by commuters in travelling longer distances, the cost of crime perpetration and prevention, the loss of income due to the more frequent occurrence of some diseases or accidents in urban centres, etc. Relevant figures, as far as they are available, show that, *inter alia,* the waste of productive resources and the level of environmental pollution are approaching the ecosystem's limits of endurance. Such factors constitute the objective and quantifiable segment of the cost of economic growth. At the same time, however, modern man's life is being debased by the pursuit of aims lying beyond his physical and mental powers. This suggests the existence of a close link between the quantifiable and the non-quantifiable aspects of social welfare, the latter relating mainly to the deterioration of the quality of life.

Among the numerous factors that are present both in the quantifiable and in the qualitative aspects of social welfare is the social cost of pollution. In the former sense, this can be appraised as the cost incurred in combating the harmful effects of pollution on human health, the physical environment, etc. In the latter sense, however, it may be said to concern all those feelings of stress and dissatisfaction that are associated with the deterioration of the environment. Such feelings are aroused when, for example, a community sees the beauty of a nearby seacoast being destroyed by industrial effluents. Furthermore, local inhabitants are probably deeply concerned at the possible adverse effects of pollution on their personal health. This condition of stress and anxiety, which is so typical of our times, is a highly significant aspect of social cost, over and above any actual or potential quantitative assessment. It is obvious that this condition is associated not only with pollution, but with a wide range of today's socio-economic phenomena. For instance, mental stress is also caused by the size and complexity of modern cities and the impersonal way of life they impose on their inhabitants. At the same time, distress and anxiety due to the rising crime wave are fundamental aspects of life in today's affluent societies.

It may therefore be said that, despite spectacular progress, modern civilisation has failed to free man of toil and fear. Instead, through its side-effects, it seems to be increasingly imprisoning the human soul in stress and anxiety. By implication, everything which is associated with the existence of external side-effects comes to be summed up at the qualitative level in the dissatisfaction of an individual forced to live a debased life; just as it is summed up in the psychological stress which suggests that the attitude of *toujours plus* does not give man the ability to enjoy the fruits of his labour. On the contrary, modern consumer societies are prone to a general deterioration of both the physical and the social environment and of human relations. Thus the individual member of the affluent society has not managed to increase his happiness correspondingly; nor has he been able to prosper at the lowest possible cost in terms of time, resources, environmental deterioration and estrangement of his own personality.

III. THE SCOPE OF THE PRESENT ESSAY

The idea that the production of more goods does not necessarily lead to a better life has begun to be appreciated by private individuals and by society as a whole. In fact, it has been observed that the relationship between social welfare and economic growth is directly associated with the stage of development in which a society finds itself. The following typology of the stages of economic development is based on the conventional distinction between inherent and socially conditioned wants. It must be emphasised, however, that this distinction is largely notional, since no clear-cut demarcation line can be drawn in practice between different types of wants. The view adopted in this study is that, in the early stages of industrialisation, the need to satisfy inherent wants was felt more urgently by the vast majority of the people, while in later stages the accent was shifted on to socially conditioned wants.

Thus, after the initial shock inflicted during the early phase of primary accumulation, when social welfare may have declined owing to a sharp change in the way of life of a large segment of the population wherever this accumulation took place, the industrial revolution has gradually led to considerable improvements.

The stage of economic growth characterised by such trends may conventionally be called, in contrast to today's affluent societies, the *society of privation*. During that period, which must have been dominated by absolute wants, each increment in national income led to a larger increase in social welfare.

As living standards improved, however, absolute wants were progressively satisfied and their importance gradually diminished. This resulted in lower rates of increase in social welfare, initially owing to saturation. At the same time, various social cost components, such as pollution and the destruction of the environment, kept growing and led to a further slowdown of the pace at which social welfare improved in response to given income increases. The ultimate outcome of this evolutionary process is the affluent society. In this phase, in which modern mature economies find them-

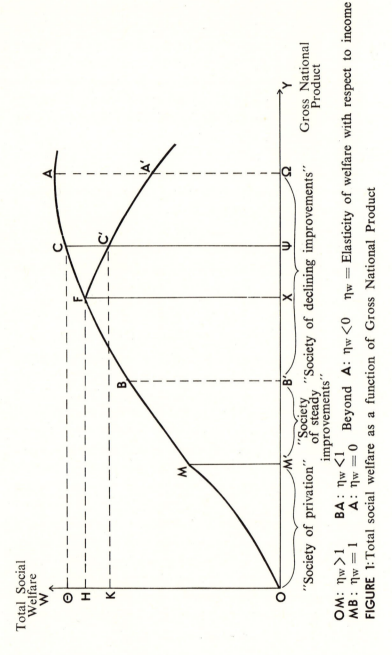

FIGURE 1: Total social welfare as a function of Gross National Product

selves at a more or less advanced stage, successive percentage increases in material output are linked to ever smaller incremental changes in social welfare, tending to become zero.

The relationship existing between economic growth during its various stages and total social welfare may be illustrated as in Figure 1. It has been mentioned that in the phase of the society of privation and after the shock of primary accumulation, every increment in the national product was translated into a larger percentage increase in social welfare. At that stage (segment OM of the OMBA curve) where absolute wants prevailed, it may be argued that the *elasticity* of social welfare in relation to the economic growth variable was higher than unity.

As a society moved further away from the state of privation, however, tendencies towards diminishing rates of increase in welfare began to prevail. This appears after point M on the OMBA curve, the farthest point being A, which denotes that the society has now reached an advanced level of affluence.

During the phase depicted by segment MB percentage increases in national product were accompanied by equal percentage increases in social welfare; the elasticity of social welfare with respect to income was equal to one. This may be called the *society of steady improvements and enjoyments.* After point B, the rate of increase in social welfare with respect to income growth diminishes, reaching zero at A (bliss point). This obviously means that in highly developed industrial economies the social benefit of economic growth tends to equal its effective social cost.

After point A, any effort to maintain the growth standards of the past may simply lead to negative rates of change in social welfare. This is so because, from that point onwards, the actual cost structure inherent in the process of sustained growth, together with the inevitable adverse psychological syndrome of diminishing well-being (owing to saturation and anxiety), is larger and increases at a faster pace than the positive social welfare factors. Consequently, in the segment after point A on the OMBA curve, the elasticity of social welfare in relation to the economic growth variable becomes negative.

The above discussion was made on the assumption of *ceteris paribus,* so that the curve representing the economic aspects of social welfare broadly expresses the total social welfare function as well. However, apart from the functional relationship between the economic aspects of welfare and the economic growth variable, various parametric changes take place in affluent societies during the process of further economic growth; such changes may even become apparent before the bliss point of the initial functional relationship is reached. In Figure 1, parametric changes are activated at point F, which represents an advanced level of affluence, though lower than A. After point F the identical evolution in total social welfare and its economic aspects breaks down. Parametric changes of this kind occur when, for instance, there is a change in the distribution of income and wealth or when the quality of life deteriorates substantially, which is obviously the case in affluent societies. This is exactly what is depicted in the graph: after point F, which relates to income level X, continuing economic growth from X to Ψ causes a severe deterioration in the quality of life. The effect of such parametric change is that the curve of total social welfare, which was so far identical with the curve of its economic aspects, undergoes a corresponding parallel shift downwards, equal to CC'.

According to the initial functional relationship which is depicted by movements along the OMBA curve from point F to point C, an increase in output or private consumption by $X\Psi$ leads to a smaller but still positive increment (HΘ) in both total social welfare and its economic aspects. In the case of a parametric shift, however, the following two forces come into play: *First,* the economic aspects of social welfare improve by HΘ. This change is shown along the initial OMBA curve. *Second,* the qualitative aspects of social welfare deteriorate. This is shown as a parametric downward shift of the initial social welfare curve by CC′=ΘK.

The final outcome of these two movements is a decrease in total social welfare by HK. This decrease is smaller than the total deterioration, ΘK, of the quality-of-life aspects of welfare, to the extent that the economic aspects of welfare continue to improve, even though at a diminishing rate. The rate, of course, corresponds to the slope — still positive — of the OMBA curve in its segment FC.

As society comes closer to the bliss point, however, the negative change in total social welfare tends to be fully identified with the rate of deterioration of the qualitative aspects of social welfare, so long as the elasticity of the economic aspects of welfare in relation to the economic growth variable tends towards zero. That is, as the bliss point is approached, there is actually no increase along the OMBA curve to offset part of the parametric shift/deterioration.

It is self-understood that, after the point where parametric forces come into play, any further increase in output leads to successive parallel downward shifts of the total social welfare curve, which finally takes the form of the curve OMFC′A′. Points C′, A′ denote successive decrements in total social welfare corresponding to increments (XΨ, ΨΩ) in GNP.

After this brief exposition of the problems involved in the process of advanced industrialisation, the object of the present essay is apparent: *first,* to examine the hypothesis that affluent societies are already at the stage of diminishing social welfare, where improvements in the economic aspects of welfare, corresponding to given increments in GNP, are systematically smaller and tend towards zero.

Second, to show — after considering the impact of parametric changes which occur at advanced stages of economic
growth — that stagnation or even negative changes in total
social welfare come before the optimal level of the economic
aspects of welfare is attained; the latter of course being
indicated by the initial functional relationship between the
economic aspects of welfare and the variable of economic
growth. Consequently, the qualitative investigation of the
matter leads to the conclusion that the negative effects of
economic growth make themselves felt more rapidly in total
welfare. This can be so, even when the economic aspects of
welfare viewed in isolation keep improving, albeit at a diminishing rate.

This essay, which is in effect an overall cost-benefit
analysis of the growth effort, uses the United States of
America as a case-study. The analysis covers the period
from 1950 to 1977. The United States has been chosen not
because it is the only country with pronounced side-effects
in the vigorous pursuit of economic growth — other mature
industrial economies functioning either according to the
laws of the free market system or even, *mutatis mutandis,*
according to a centrally planned system, may exhibit similar symptoms — but simply because the statistical material
available for the United States is relatively more abundant
regarding both the economic aspects of welfare and purely
qualitative factors. Also, the United States has been chosen
because, to a large extent, it is a closed economy and this
enhances the significance of certain trends that were observed
in that period and may therefore be regarded as inherent.
Lastly, the choice of the period from 1950 to 1977 is based
on the belief that during that time the United States was
transformed into an affluent society. However, wherever
possible, comparable data are also given for a number of
selected countries at an advanced level of affluence.

APPENDIX TO CHAPTER ONE

The foregoing discussion is depicted in the following functional relationship:[18]

(1) $W = f(Y, \overline{Z}, \overline{X})$

where: W = total social welfare

Y = per capita income (or private consumption)

$\overline{Z}$ = distributional aspects of welfare

$\overline{X}$ = quality-of-life aspects of welfare

For the moment, Z and X are treated as parametric constants, which are activated at advanced stages of economic growth. Obviously, if this assumption is valid (namely, so long as Z and X are considered constants of the relationship being examined), W no longer denotes total social welfare but becomes merely an indicator of the economic aspects of it. It is reasonable to assume, however, that in earlier stages of capitalistic development, this magnitude was a satisfactory indicator of total social welfare.

To show the historical progress of social welfare through the life-cycle of economic development, it is necessary to consider two factors, which operate with lesser or greater relative intensity according to the level of social welfare already attained. These factors are distinguished into a factor of momentum (impulse factor) and a retarding factor.

The greater the distance between the actual level of social welfare and its potential maximum level (point of bliss), the greater the effect of the impulse factor. On the other hand, as a society approaches the point of bliss, retarding forces come into play. In the present phase of economic development in the industrial nations, the retarding factor is relatively stronger, with the result of constantly lengthening the time required for a society to rise from an already very high actual level of social welfare to the bliss point. These thoughts can be expressed in the following differential equation:

$$(2) \quad \frac{dW}{dY} = \underset{\substack{\uparrow \\ \text{Impulse} \\ \text{factor}}}{kW} \quad \underset{\substack{\text{Retarding} \\ \text{factor}}}{\underbrace{(A - W)}}$$

where: k is the proportionality coefficient
A = the point of bliss
W = the actual level of social welfare.

Attainment of the point of bliss would be determined by a variety of factors; namely by the actual distribution of national income and wealth, the extent of environmental pollution, the extent to which and the rate at which natural resources are being depleted, or even by the psychological saturation of the members of a typical affluent society.

In the extreme case where A = W, (2) gives $\frac{dW}{dY} = 0,$ which means that beyond this point, any further increase in income is futile.

By integrating (2) and performing the standard manipulations, the specific functional form of (1) is obtained as equation (11) in the following sequence.

Equation (2) may be rewritten as follows:

$$(3) \quad \frac{1}{W(A-W)} \cdot dW = k \cdot dY \quad \text{or:}$$

$$(4) \quad \frac{1}{A} \left(\frac{1}{W} + \frac{1}{A-W} \right) dW = k \cdot dY$$

Integration of (4) gives:

$$(5) \quad \int \left(\frac{1}{W} + \frac{1}{A-W} \right) \cdot dW = A \cdot k \int dY$$

$$(6) \quad \ln W - \ln (A-W) = AkY + D$$

where D is a constant. (6) can be written in the form:

$$(7) \quad \ln \frac{W}{A-W} = AkY + D \quad \text{or:}$$

(8) $\dfrac{W}{A-W} = e^{AkY + D}$

The reciprocal of (8) gives:

(9) $A-W = We^{-AkY} \cdot e^{-D}$

Setting $Ak = C$ and $e^{-D} = B$,
equation (9) becomes:

(10) $A-W = We^{-CY} \cdot B$

Solving for W, we obtain:

(11) $W = \dfrac{A}{1 + Be^{-CY}}$

If time-series were available for W and Y, and for the whole history of the industrial system, it would be possible to compute coefficients A, B and C with the help of non-linear econometric methods. It would then be possible to investigate the stages that the society in question has gone through, the point at which it now stands, and how far this is from the point where it becomes $A=W$.

If $Y \to \infty$, then $e^{-CY} \to 0$ and $W = A$. The bliss point in function (11) is attained asymptotically at very high income levels.

Figure 1 depicts the situation that prevails when the variables Z, X (namely the distributional and non-economic aspects of welfare) are assumed as parametric constants.

If this assumption is relaxed, however, and especially if it is accepted that the quality-of-life aspects of welfare deteriorate at advanced levels of economic growth, then from this point onwards the social welfare curve undergoes successive parallel shifts downwards (see F C′ A′). This of course depicts the effect of the above-mentioned negative factors. Thus owing to parametric shifts, it becomes impossible to attain the original bliss point. Furthermore, in the above case the decrease in the level of social welfare corresponding to given increases in income relates to the extent of the shift of the social welfare curve, before any such movement is suggested by the initial functional relationship.

The foregoing analysis does not look into the entire historical process of capital accumulation and growth and its effects on total social welfare during the period of industrialisation. Rather, it intends to examine the last 25 to 30 years, which correspond to the last segment of the logistic curve that relates to the affluent society.

NOTES

TO INTRODUCTION AND CHAPTER ONE

1. J. K. Galbraith defines an affluent society by saying that in such a society "unlimited" possibilities press on "limited" needs.

2. Harrison Brown, "Population Growth and Affluence: The Fissioning of Human Society," *Quarterly Journal of Economics*, May 1975.

3. The industrial nations' target is to provide 0.7 per cent of their annual GNP as aid to the countries of the Third World by 1985. For the time being, the developed countries' annual outlays for development assistance total $20 billion, a very small sum indeed, compared with the amount of $400 billion spent on armaments (*North-South: A Program for Survival*, Report of the Independent Commission on International Development Issues, The MIT Press, 1980, pp. 269-78).

Typical of prevailing trends is also the fact that "in 1949, at the beginning of the Marshall Plan, U.S. Official Development Assistance amounted to 2.79 per cent of GNP. Today, it is less than one-tenth of that: 0.22 per cent of GNP. And this after a quarter century during which the income of the average American, adjusted for inflation, has more than doubled." (Robert S. McNamara, *Development and the Arms Race*, University of Chicago, May 22, 1979, p. 6.)

4. During the first industrial revolution, say from approximately 1750 to 1850, technology relied mainly on artisan organisation and was the outcome of practical experience rather than scientific knowledge. By contrast, the second industrial revolution, which had its beginnings in the 1850s, relied on technological achievements based on scientific discoveries (Orio Giarini, *Dialogue on Wealth and Welfare – An Alternative View of World Capital Formation*, Pergamon Press, 1980, pp. 74-75).

5. The extent to which modern technology is energy-consuming is evident from the fact that the United States, with its enormous technological progress, accounts for roughly one-third of the world's annual energy consumption, despite having only 5.5 per cent of the earth's population (John Holdren, "Technology, Environment, and Well-Being: Some Critical Choices," in *Growth in America,* ed. Chester L. Cooper, Green Wood Press, 1976, p. 101). Regarding material-intensity, the same book mentions Harrison Brown's calculations, according to which output of industrial metals would

have to be sixty times larger than in 1970 to provide the world population of 1970 with the capital stock of industrial metals, per person, that prevailed in 1970 in the ten richest countries (*ibid.,* p. 95).

Specifically for the United States, it is estimated that the quantity of materials consumed outside the construction sector amounts to thirteen tons per capita annually (*Fortune,* February 1970). Furthermore, the average U.S. citizen's dependence on modern technology is such that the various products, appliances, etc. incorporating advanced technology supply every man, woman and child in the United States with services equivalent to the muscular power of five hundred "servants" (*ibid.*). Aristotle cannot have had exactly such a future in mind when he wrote, about two thousand years ago, that the day would come when tools would replace human labour and that when that happened, artisans would no longer need labourers, nor masters their slaves (*Politics,* Book 1, Chapter 3).

At the root of the negative aspects of modern technology is the fact that technological progress is largely the outcome of research carried out in the laboratories of the arms industry. The dependence of modern technology on the arms industry is impressive if we consider that research in this field absorbs more funds worldwide than the fields of energy, health, education and food combined. Public expenditures on weapons research and development approach $30 billion a year and mobilise the talents of half a million scientists and engineers throughout the world. Global defence expenditures are now in excess of $400 billion a year, the two superpowers (United States and the Soviet Union) together accounting for more than half of the world's total defence bill, and for some two-thirds of the world's arms trade (McNamara, *op. cit.*).

6. "The historical record gives us reason to be optimistic that innovation of a resource-augmenting nature will continue. There is no known limit on possible improvements in technology, although the possibility of diminishing returns to research and development has been raised." (Charles W. Howe, *Natural Resource Economics: Issues, Analysis and Policy,* John Wiley & Sons, 1979, p. 13.)

7. Bertrand de Jouvenel describes our times as the *civilisation de toujours plus.* From "Organisation du travail et l'aménagement de l'existence", *Free University Quarterly,* VII (August 1959).

8. "Increases in productivity allow for higher standards of living and the legitimation of advanced capitalism... As long as growth based on limitless capital accumulation is possible, the problem of exploitation and the distribution of the social product ceases to be a political or class problem."

(Stephen Rousseas, *Capitalism and Catastrophe*, Cambridge University Press, 1979, pp. 6-7.)

9. "Capitalism is the first mode of production in world history to institutionalise self-sustaining growth." (Jürgen Habermas, *Toward a Rational Society: Student Protest, Science, and Politics*, Boston, 1970, p. 96.)

10. Adam Smith, *The Wealth of Nations*, New York, The Modern Library, 1937, p. 81.

11. The matter is discussed thoroughly by William J. Baumol and Wallace E. Oates in *Economics, Environmental Policy and the Quality of Life*, (Englewood Cliffs, N. J., Prentice-Hall, 1979, pp. 80 and 91). Among other things, Baumol and Oates note that "...governmental ownership and central planning do not automatically do away with the abuse of a society's natural resources and its quality of life. State enterprises, just like private firms, may find it easiest to pour their liquid wastes into the nearest waterway and to emit their fumes into the atmosphere... We must, therefore, be prepared to look to one another for fruitful ideas and effective programs, and we must not be deterred by the labels of measures as 'bourgeois' or 'socialistic'."

12. Similarly to Smith, Ricardo and Malthus painted a gloomy picture of the stationary state. On the same question, the opinion held by McCulloch is typical (see John Stuart Mill, *Principles of Political Economy*, ed. Sir William Ashley, London, Longmans, 1909. [Reprinted, Clifton, N. J., Augustus M. Kelley, 1973, p. 747.]) In his view, prosperity is associated not with increased output and the fair distribution of wealth, but with the rate of increase in the latter or, to use modern terms, with the rate of economic growth. According to McCulloch, when profits — the factor underlying the rate of increase in wealth (the rate of economic growth) — are falling, the rate of economic growth also falls and so does economic welfare.

13. "I confess I am not charmed with the ideal of life held out by those who think that the normal state of human beings is that of struggling to get on... It is only in the backward countries of the world that increased production is still an important object: in those most advanced, what is economically needed is a better distribution... It is scarcely necessary to remark that a stationary condition of capital and population implies no stationary state of human improvement. There would be as much scope as ever for all kinds of mental culture, and moral and social progress; as much room for improving the Art of Living..." (*ibid.*, pp. 748, 749 and 751).

Concerning Mill's attitude, Joseph A. Schumpeter in his *History of Economic Analysis*, (London, Allen & Unwin, 1954, p. 571), very correctly observes that Mill appears to be more optimistic than Smith and Ricardo, because he removes the spectre of overpopulation from his analysis.

Alfred Marshall also did not accept that only money or the possession of material wealth must be the pivot of economic science: "Thus, though it is true that 'money' or 'general purchasing power' or 'command over material wealth', is the centre around which economic science clusters; this is so, not because money or material wealth is regarded as the main aim of human effort, nor even as affording the main subject-matter for the study of the economist... If the older economists had made this clear, they... would not then have been marred by bitter attacks... based on the mistaken belief that science had no concern with any motive except the selfish desire for wealth..." (Alfred Marshall, *Principles of Economics*, London, Macmillan, 1952, pp. 18-19).

14. The secular trend towards the stationary state was indirectly acknowledged by John Maynard Keynes too, who held that it would come about gradually, when "capital ceases to be scarce", through the socialisation of the investment function. In his *General Theory of Employment, Interest and Money* (London, Macmillan, 1946, pp. 375-78), Keynes says: "This state of affairs... would mean the euthanasia of the rentier, and, consequently, the euthanasia of the cumulative oppressive power of the capitalist to exploit the scarcity-value of capital... I see, therefore, the rentier aspect of capitalism as a transitional phase which will disappear when it has done its work... I conceive, therefore, that a somewhat comprehensive socialisation of investment will prove the only means of securing an approximation to full employment."

15. Consumerism, as used in the text, means overconsumption; it should therefore be distinguished from any movement tending to safeguard consumers' interests.

16. "But... [needs] fall into two classes — those needs which are absolute in the sense that we feel them whatever the situation of our fellow human beings may be, and those which are relative in the sense that we feel them only if their satisfaction lifts us above, makes us feel superior to, our fellows. Needs of the second class, those which satisfy the desire for superiority, may indeed be insatiable." (*The Collected Writings of John Maynard Keynes*, Vol. IX, *Essays in Persuasion*, London, Macmillan, 1972, p. 326.)

17. Many electronic devices, such as video sets, cameras, pocket calculators, are so complex that most people use only a limited range of their capacity or alternative applications.

18. The appendix contains an analytic approach related to the discussion on the scope of this essay. It will be seen, however, that according to this analysis total social welfare tends only asymptotically to a maximum as per capita income grows.

CHAPTER TWO

THE TOTAL SOCIAL
WELFARE FUNCTION

From the time of the classical economists until a few years ago, economic development — the increase in the "wealth of nations" as expressed through increases in the national product — was regarded by the majority of economists as the most reliable indicator of an improvement in the prosperity and well-being of a nation. This view was based on the tacit assumption — a very sound one for the age of absolute wants — that the elimination of poverty should be the principal aim of any effort to improve the overall standard of living. An increase in per capita national product was then equivalent to an increase in social welfare. So long as economic activity was closely associated with the improvement of social welfare, no distinction could be made between positive economics and the economics of welfare. Even the name of the science was Political Economy, which, as Adam Smith put it, was "considered as a branch of the science of a statesman or legislator".[1]

The distinction between positive economics and the economics of welfare began to emerge in the mid-1920s and was based on the line drawn by the positivist school between objective truths and subjective valuations. While in positive economics one could test the conclusion of a theory against reality to see if the theory was correct, in welfare economics only the assumptions can be subjected to some kind of "test"; the conclusions are of a normative character.[2]

In this essay, the notion of social welfare is considered in a general sense so as to include, in addition to economic variables, every other interdependence that directly or indirectly affects man's well-being. Accordingly, total social welfare is examined as a function of economic progress, with special reference to advanced stages of economic growth.[3] In this sense, the social welfare function includes not only factors that directly determine the economic aspects of social welfare, but also non economic factors which, together with the distributional aspects of welfare, determine overall social well-being. Economic growth, when used as a proxy for social welfare, is not only unnecessarily restrictive, but may also be a misleading indicator of it, at least as far as the advanced industrial economies are concerned. The earliest concept of one-to-one correspondence between economic growth and social welfare was generally correct and in line with the historical developments that helped shape it during the Age of Great Discoveries and the New Frontier ideology. But things have changed radically since then. So much so, that the attainment of high growth levels cannot tell the whole story and the growth potential is no longer unlimited. What is needed today is a more general assessment of the weighted costs and benefits of economic growth in contemporary advanced societies, together with clearly stated normative criteria in making economic policy decisions.[4]

As a first step towards the formation of a general notion of social welfare, its economic aspects are examined in isolation.[5] They are not identified, however, only with private consumption or gross national product; additional elements of social costs and benefits are taken into consideration. This is done because, in general, national income accounts disregard basic social cost components, such as external diseconomies, the cost of induced obsolescence, etc. The omission of such elements renders national income statistics more or less biased indicators of the economic aspects of social welfare.

Externalities, whether positive or negative, cause a divergence between private and social costs and benefits respectively. As a result, the equilibrium of private markets can be suboptimal from the social welfare standpoint. The reason is that the diseconomies which are "internalised" in the social welfare function are not taken into account in calculating private production costs and benefits. If private cost were to include externalities in general — whether positive or negative — the production optimum determined by private optimality criteria would approximate the social optimum, so that national income accounts would reflect more faithfully the effective social cost of output.

Pollution and the deterioration of the physical and human environment are the main side-effects experienced by highly industrialised societies, which have to be taken into account in the formulation of a social welfare function. A related item, which is also omitted from national income accounts, is the cost of urbanisation. This includes, among other things, the social cost involved in the systematic lengthening of the distance between the place of residence and the place of work, as well as the continuous deterioration of the quality of life in major urban centres. Moreover, to make a function expressing the economic aspects of social welfare meaningful in the context of today's problems, it has to include the very high social cost involved in the wasteful use of natural resources, both renewable and non-renewable. This question is particularly relevant in view of the progressively deepening energy crisis.

By contrast, national income accounts record the value of intermediate or corrective goods and services. The latter, though they do not promote social welfare, aim usually at counteracting any harm done during the process of economic growth. It is thus reasonable to exclude all such goods and services from a measurement of economic welfare.[6]

Apart from this far from exhaustive listing of the principal components of social cost, there are some very significant aspects of social benefit, which also fail to find their way into national income accounts. These are basically items of a non-market character and, to the extent they are affected by the process of economic growth, they have a varying effect on social welfare. The main items of this kind, which are analysed in detail in the third chapter, are household services (or housework) and leisure time.

Housework is affected by economic growth in such a way that, beyond a certain point, the corresponding level of income becomes an upward biased indicator of economic welfare. This is because conventional practice was not to count housework in the national product. This item, though, is practically included in more recent series of the national accounts, to the extent that it is replaced by the services of durable household goods, as well as the various services offered in the market (dry-cleaning stores, laundries, etc.) and reckoned as items of GNP. Regarding leisure time, it has to be determined first of all whether this magnitude, which is vital from the standpoint of social welfare, increases, decreases or remains the same as a result of economic growth; then, the imputed value of free time is regarded as a positive item in the social welfare function.

What has been said so far relates to the first part of this essay, which concerns the impact of economic growth on social welfare; namely, it relates to the construction of an index of the economic aspects of welfare which, by providing the fullest possible information on effective social cost-benefit aspects, would be a better approximation than GNP, which is often used as a *de facto* indicator of economic welfare. The view taken in this essay is that, when due consider-

ation is given to the interplay between economic growth
and the economic aspects of social welfare, the latter increases at a slower pace than economic growth as measured
in the national accounts.

In the second part, an attempt is made to examine the
effects of economic growth on the qualitative aspects of
social welfare. The underlying ethical principle is that
people of the same temperament have a comparable ability
to enjoy the fruits of welfare. The acceptance of this principle presumes that the policy-maker is fully aware of the
overall effects on social well-being of any decision which is
seemingly associated only with economic variables. Accordingly, the choice to allocate public resources for, say, the
development of a recreational area in a highly polluted
industrial zone is much more important than the alternative
choice to build a tennis court in some spotlessly clean
suburb. The reasoning is that environmental pollution exerts
an important qualitative influence, besides the narrowly economic one which the index of the economic aspects of welfare
attempts to quantify. It is the state of anguish that the population falls into when it sees the beauty of the surroundings
in which it lives and works deteriorating, or the feeling
of stress and deep anxiety experienced with regard to the
possible effects of pollution on children's health, etc. This
reasoning is based on the ethical consideration that the population of the hypothetical industrial zone has precisely the
same ability to enjoy and appreciate clean air, natural beauty
and healthy living conditions as the inhabitants of the high-
income suburb. Assuming that this argument is valid, it is
then logical to infer that total social welfare would be
enhanced much more if the first alternative were chosen
rather than the second.[7]

The foregoing example is related to the much broader
question of external diseconomies; in this case, to the non-

quantifiable aspect of environmental pollution leading to a
deterioration of the quality of life. It is also related to the
way in which a debased life is "distributed" among the
various groups forming a community. It is along these lines
that it is attempted to identify the effects of economic growth
on the qualitative aspects of social welfare. The implication
of the biblical dictum "man shall not live by bread alone"
is that human beings cannot live by satisfying merely material needs; man must also be in harmony with himself
and with his natural environment if he is to attain happiness
and prosperity. An individual should have the chance to
satisfy his intellectual and aesthetic aspirations by being able
to give an outlet to his creative desires and aptitudes. To do
so, however, he has to be free of the mental stress caused
to a large extent by the ecological disharmonies prevailing
in today's advanced societies.

When economists of the classical tradition asserted that
a nation was prospering, their notion of prosperity en-
compassed the whole range of human activities, including
elements not directly related to economic activity, which were
implicitly regarded as given and immutable. In those days,
economic development was a necessary and sufficient condition for an improvement in total social welfare. In Adam
Smith's time, for instance, the foremost prerequisite for an
improvement in living conditions was an increase in the
national product. During the period of primary accumulation, the working class lived in abject misery and a rise in
the national product was a *conditio sine qua non* for reducing
infant mortality, improving health, housing and working
conditions, etc. Occasional environmental pollution and
deterioration was not felt at that time as the widespread
problem it is today. Consequently, it was only natural to
identify narrowly defined economic with total social welfare
and to disregard all those side-effects which grew in import-

ance during subsequent stages of development. It is precisely those variables which must be carefully analysed now that total social welfare is examined in the context of today's affluent societies.

It is understood, of course, that it is virtually impossible to quantify with any degree of precision the deterioration of the quality of life or to make interpersonal comparisons among such highly subjective factors. Nevertheless, this essay attempts to collect and depict systematically some of the principal elements that make for the quality of life and are subject to change in various degrees in the process of economic growth. It may thus be possible to obtain specific indications regarding the relationship between, for example, alcoholism or crime and urbanisation, an important phenomenon which is a direct outcome of industrial development.

NOTES

TO CHAPTER TWO

1. "Political economy, considered as a branch of the science of a statesman or legislator..." (Adam Smith, *The Wealth of Nations*, New York, The Modern Library, 1937, p. 397).

2. The academic discipline of welfare economics centres mainly around the soundness of the normative criticism expressed by economists. Until a few years ago, the prevailing attitude was that of "scientific neutrality", which was supported by the advocates of Pareto's school of thought and their descendants. The Paretian concept presumes given consumer tastes, a given distribution of income and the absence of externalities. According to Pareto, the notion of social welfare is a strictly logical construction. Social welfare is "a monotonic increasing function of individual welfare" (see S. K. Nath, *A Reappraisal of Welfare Economics*, London, Routledge and Kegan Paul, 1969, p. 127), in which the question of the relativity of the individual functions composing it does not arise. Consequently, there is no information concerning those cases in which an economic change improves the position of some people, but worsens — either absolutely or comparatively — the position of others. Also, no light is shed on the situation, when the level of satisfaction of some members of society is altered by the concurrence of external economies.

The Paretian principle of scientific neutrality was developed mainly through the Hicks-Slutsky consumer demand theory, which became the basic reference point in the literature during the three decades or so after the publication of Hicks's *Value and Capital*. On the other hand, Pigou was the first to do away with academic reservations concerning the issue of interpersonal comparisons, by arguing that all people of the same basic psychological make-up have the same ability to enjoy the fruits of welfare, the same ability to enjoy life. By allowing his analysis to consider distributional aspects and the effects of externalities, Pigou's *Economics of Welfare* thus paved the way for a broader view of the social welfare function, which was later formulated by A. Bergson in "A Reformulation of Certain Aspects of Welfare Economics" (*Quarterly Journal of Economics,* 1938).

3. The total social welfare function cannot be regarded as consisting of separate segments of welfare (economic, political, aesthetic, etc.), because in actual fact it is a single and indivisible whole. "There is no part of

well-being called 'economic well-being'. The word 'economic' qualifies not well-being, but the causes of well-being or changes in it. If I am interested only in someone's economic welfare, then I interest myself only in the economic things which may affect his well-being." (I.M.D. Little, *A Critique of Welfare Economics*, 2nd ed., London, Oxford University Press, 1965, p. 6.) Hence, the term "social welfare function", where used for the sake of brevity, should be interpreted as the "total social welfare function." Similarly, the term "economic welfare" denotes the economic aspects of social welfare or rather the economic factors affecting social welfare.

4. We are aware of the difficulties involved in identifying the effects (economic and non-economic) and attaching to them the proper weights in any cost-benefit analysis. In the present case, the difficulties are compounded by the extent of the research field. Nonetheless, we have deemed it worth the effort, though the results of the calculations are of course approximations.

5. In this essay, the distribution of income and wealth is considered to be given. The reason is that, in the specific case of the United States after the Second World War, there are no clear indications of substantial changes in the existing pattern of income distribution. There are various views concerning the relationship between economic development and income distribution. Simon Kuznets argues that there is an improvement in the distribution of income, before direct taxes and governmental transfers, in the industrialised economies. According to Kuznets: "The data... for the United States, England and Germany... suggested... that the relative distribution of income, as measured by annual income incidence in rather broad classes, has been moving toward equality with these trends particularly noticeable since the 1920's but beginning perhaps in the period before the First World War... One might thus assume a long swing in the inequality characterizing the secular income structure: widening in the early phases of economic growth when the transition from the pre-industrial to the industrial civilization was most rapid; becoming stabilized for a while; and then narrowing in the later phases." (S. Kuznets, "Economic Growth and Income Inequality," *American Economic Review*, Vol. XLV, [March 1955], pp. 4 and 18. [Reprinted in B. Okun and R. W. Richardson, *Studies in Economic Development*, New York, Holt, Rinehart, Winston, 1964.])

Kuznets's essay primed a whole series of research papers aimed at an empirical verification of his "inverted U hypothesis." (See H. Chenery and M. Syrquin, *Patterns of Development, 1950-1970,* London, Oxford University Press, 1975. Also, M. Ahluwalia, "Inequality, Poverty and Development," *Journal of Development Economics,* [December 1976], pp. 307-342;

P. Roberti, "Income Distribution : A Time-Series and a Cross-Section Study," *The Economic Journal*, Vol. 84, [September 1974], pp. 629-38.) Most of these studies relied on cross-section data to investigate differences in income inequality among countries at different levels of economic development. Broadly speaking, the results of these studies confirmed the position taken by Kuznets. The matter is less clear, however, in studies based on time-series data relating to recent developments in income inequality in countries already at an advanced stage of industrialisation. On this point, P. Roberti ("Income Distribution: A Time-Series and a Cross-Section Study", *op. cit.,* p. 633) concludes that one must be reserved in the interpretation of overall coefficients that suggest a decreasing income inequality in the process of economic growth. "... The previous analysis of the trends in the income shares of the different deciles suggests that we should be suspicious of the evidence given by overall coefficients. These are known to produce inconsistent and misleading results and this seems to be the present case for which we have seen no 'consistent' change."

Specific reference is made to the United States, where income distribution is of particular interest because, if a substantial improvement/deterioration has occurred, the total social welfare index must be adjusted accordingly. Roberti's study shows that between 1947 and 1970 the income share of the top decile of the population decreased from 28.1 per cent to 24.7 per cent, while there was a slight increase of the 5th (from 7.7 to 7.8 per cent), 6th (from 9.2 to 9.5 per cent), 7th (from 10.9 to 11.6 per cent), 8th (from 13.0 to 13.9 per cent) and 9th deciles (from 16.5 to 18.2 per cent). For the poorer 50 per cent of the population, however, there was a slight decrease (4th decile: from 6.2 to 6.1 per cent; 3rd decile : from 4.5 to 4.3 per cent; 2nd decile: from 2.8 to 2.7 per cent), except for the bottom decile, which increased its share slightly from 1.01 to 1.08 per cent. These data do not support the view that the improvement in income distribution in the United States after World War II was significant enough to justify the hypothesis of a positive effect on the social welfare index. What seems to have occurred, according to Roberti's study, was a redistribution among the groups comprising the upper 50 per cent of the population. It seems that several other studies have reached similar conclusions. To the question "Are we better off?" in the Report of the U.S. Department of Health, Education and Welfare, the reply is that, in postwar America, income distribution has remained virtually stable. "Although overall income levels are high and rising, the distribution of income in the United States has remained practically unchanged in the last 20 years... the Depression of the 1930's brought a sharp drop in the share of the top 5 per cent of all families and unrelated individuals and a rise in the share of the lowest 20 per cent. World War II brought an even more marked rise in the share of the lowest 20 per cent. However, since the mid-1940's, there has been little observable change in the overall distribution of income. The lowest 20 per cent of households have consistently received 5 per cent or less of personal income and less than 4 per cent of total money income." (U.S. Department of Health, Education and Welfare, *Toward a Social Report,* Ann Arbor, The University of Michigan Press, 1970, p. 42.)

In this connection, Lester C. Thurow holds a more explicit view, according to which, during the period 1947-1977, the lower 60 per cent of the population (in terms of income) effectively lost part of their purchasing power, which remains unchanged at the family income level only because of governmental transfers and the high participation rates of women of these income classes in the labour force. This remark is of course relevant only as regards female labour, since most of the studies previously referred to concern the pre-tax, pre-transfer distribution of income. Nevertheless, the factor of female labour, which seems to some extent to have played a balancing role in the *ex ante* pattern of income distribution, will, in Thurow's view, cease to play this role in the future. This is because there are indications of a growing participation in the labour force of women married to men earning high incomes. Thus, "with income transfer payments slowing down and working wives contributing to inequality rather than equality, the distribution of family income will start moving toward inequality in the 1980s and 1990s." (L. Thurow, *The Zero-Sum Society*, New York, Basic Books, 1980, p. 157.)

This line of argument justifies the "neutral" stance of the present study regarding the distribution of income in the United States during the period from 1950 to 1977. For that period, the distributional aspect of welfare has been taken as a constant, with no effect on the index of social welfare.

6. Goods and services in this category are merely "antidotes", in the sense that they derive their value from the negative factor that is being countered and whose existence makes them necessary. According to Fred Hirsch, "another way of looking at consumer intermediate goods is to see them as 'defensive' goods (sometimes termed 'regrettable necessities')." (F. Hirsch, *Social Limits to Growth,* Cambridge, Mass., Harvard University Press, 1976, p. 57.)

7. This position, of course, differs basically from the value theory which was renovated by Pareto, who introduced the concept of ordinal utility in

lieu of cardinal utility. According to this theory and since utility is ordinal, the economist as such cannot rule in favour of either situation in terms of economic desirability. Thus, Economics as a value-free science was distinguished from Political Economy. In this way, however, the role of Economics was restricted; therefore, a reintegration of Economics with Political Economy was attempted, with the acceptance of value-free prescriptions, ethically neutral.

In this context, it was Kaldor who first formulated a compensation criterion later endorsed by Hicks. According to the Kaldor-Hicks criterion, value-free is not only the choice of an economic policy which results in raising the welfare of some individuals without reducing the welfare of the rest. Value-free is also any other choice which results in worsening the welfare of some people while improving the welfare of others, provided that those who gain by this specific choice can compensate those who lose so that their utility will not diminish and something will be left over for the former. In this case, the specific economic policy is both desirable and justified.

Scitovsky showed later that the Kaldor-Hicks criterion was capable of contradicting itself. To eliminate this contradiction, he proposed the so-called "Scitovsky reversal criterion". According to this criterion, assuming that those losing from a specific economic policy choice are not compensated, they should not be able to "bribe" those who gain into abstaining from this choice. This means not only that the new situation should satisfy the Kaldor-Hicks criterion, but also that a shift from the new situation to the old one should *not* satisfy this criterion.

For the above analysis see :

—N. Kaldor, "Welfare Propositions of Economics and Interpersonal Comparisons of Utility," *The Economic Journal,* Vol. XLIX (September 1939), pp. 549-52.

—J. R. Hicks, "The Foundations of Welfare Economics," *The Economic Journal,* Vol. XLIX (December 1939), pp. 696-712.

—T. Scitovsky, "A Note on Welfare Propositions in Economics," *Review of Economic Studies,* (November 1941).

CHAPTER THREE

INDEX OF THE ECONOMIC ASPECTS OF WELFARE

I. INTRODUCTORY REMARKS

In this chapter, an index of the economic aspects of welfare (the EAW-index) is constructed, depicting the full range of actual changes in a society's quantifiable well-being, regardless of whether or not these changes are the outcome of market transactions.[1] As stated previously, the GNP cannot serve this purpose because by its very nature it is a measure of the productive potential of a society and not especially of its welfare.[2] The national income accounting system of the United States, which is used as a benchmark in this research, was introduced in the thirties to provide a satisfactory description of that country's productive potential. In fact, after the financial crash of 1929 and the recovery particularly after World War II, national income accounts were confined to the task of successfully depicting fluctuations in overall economic activity. In a system of this nature, attention focuses on inputs and outputs. Thus, for instance, the value of working time, which is implicitly included in the national accounts, is regarded merely as an input which yields purchasing power, but no attention is paid to other — non-market — uses of time, such as leisure.

It should be stressed here that no attempt is made to replace the national accounts system by the EAW-index, because it is recognised that the national accounts serve a different purpose.[3]

Despite inherent difficulties and the relatively arbitrary assumptions that sometimes have to be made in calculating specific magnitudes of the EAW-index, its purpose is to depict the direction of change in the effective economic well-being of a society that is already in the stage of advanced industrialism.

II. THEORETICAL AND EMPIRICAL COMPILATION OF THE EAW-INDEX

The compilation of the EAW-index is based mainly on national income accounts and particularly on private consumption, which has the most direct bearing on a society's well-being. This is because it is assumed that an extension of the effective range of opportunities available to the members of a society serves to increase that society's economic welfare, while included in the GNP are components — such as investments — which do not directly increase economic welfare. Private consumption has therefore been used instead of GNP.

The reason for choosing private instead of total consumption is that the latter includes public sector consumption, a large part of which is considered to be of an intermediate or corrective nature.[4] Specifically, expenditures on national defence, police services, fire department activities, etc., are corrective. They serve to "purchase" goods and services essential for the preservation of fundamental social values, such as personal freedom and public order. If, for instance, there is an increase in crime in a certain district and the local authorities are forced to double outlays for police protection, this does not mean that the people living in that district now enjoy twice as much "security" as they did before. It would therefore be inappropriate to consider that such outlays increase social welfare. Moreover, public sector

consumption includes civil servants' salaries, which reappear
to a large extent on the private consumption side as demand
for goods and services by that category of citizens.

This, of course, does not mean that corrective goods and
services are completely absent from private consumption;
there are innumerable examples of corrective expenditures

TABLE 1

Gross National Product and Private Consumption

($ billion, at 1972 prices)

Year	GNP	Private consumption	Year	GNP	Private consumption
1950	533.5	338.1	1964	874.4	528.7
1951	576.5	342.3	1965	925.9	558.1
1952	598.5	350.9	1966	981.0	586.1
1953	621.8	364.2	1967	1,007.7	603.2
1954	613.7	370.9	1968	1,051.8	633.4
1955	654.8	395.1	1969	1,078.8	655.4
1956	668.8	406.3	1970	1,075.3	668.9
1957	680.9	414.7	1971	1,107.5	691.9
1958	679.5	419.0	1972	1,171.1	733.0
1959	720.4	441.5	1973	1,235.0	767.7
1960	736.8	453.0	1974	1,217.8	760.7
1961	755.3	462.2	1975	1,202.3	774.6
1962	799.1	482.9	1976	1,271.0	819.4
1963	830.7	501.4	1977	1,332.7	857.7

Source : Economic Report of the President, U.S. Government Printing
Office, Washington, D.C., 1979, p. 184.

on the part of private individuals. Purchases of tranquil-
lisers, for instance, represent a largely corrective expenditure, since the need for such drugs is aggravated by the
contemporary neurotic way of life. Nevertheless, since corrective expenditures in the private sector (e.g. pharmaceuticals, hand-guns, alarm systems, safety locks etc.) seem to be
low in comparison with the corresponding category of public

expenditure, no effort has been made to quantify them in the
process of compiling the EAW-index.

The use of private consumption as a basic framework
for the compilation of the EAW-index therefore appears to be
justified. There are of course certain public sector expenditures, such as health and education, which directly promote
social welfare. Despite their origin (government budget),

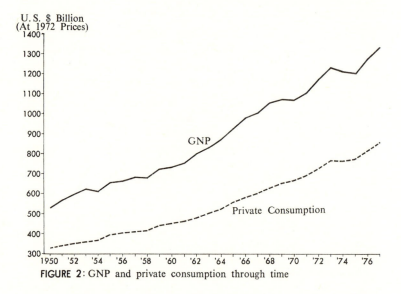

FIGURE 2: GNP and private consumption through time

such expenditures must be incorporated in the index, along
with the services which society receives year after year from
the existing stock of "public capital" (mainly public buildings). To the extent that these services add to social welfare, they should be part of the index.

In compiling the EAW-index, various other magnitudes
are added to or deducted from private consumption according to whether they are positively or negatively related to
economic welfare and according to whether they vary as a
result of the economic growth process.

1. Items Deducted from Private Consumption for a Closer Approximation to the EAW-Index

(a) Durable consumer goods

Private expenditure on consumer durables (Table 2) is deducted from private consumption. The reason is that consumers do not enjoy their services all at once, but rather gradually and in accordance with the flow of such

TABLE 2

Private Expenditure on Durable Consumer Goods

(At 1972 prices)

Year	$ billion	Year	$ billion	Year	$ billion
1950	43.4	1960	52.5	1970	88.9
1951	39.9	1961	50.3	1971	98.1
1952	38.9	1962	55.7	1972	111.2
1953	43.1	1963	60.7	1973	121.8
1954	43.5	1964	65.7	1974	112.5
1955	52.2	1965	73.4	1975	112.7
1956	49.8	1966	79.0	1976	125.9
1957	49.7	1967	79.7	1977	137.8
1958	46.4	1968	88.2		
1959	51.8	1969	91.9		

Source : Economic Report of the President, U.S. Government Printing Office, Washington, D.C., 1979, p. 184.

services over a period of time.[5] Therefore, the EAW-index includes the annual flows of services derived from this class of goods over their estimated useful life span, as described in greater detail in the appropriate section of this chapter.

(b) Advertising

There exist several intermediate goods and services, the use or rather abuse of which fails to contribute, even

TABLE 3

Advertising Expenditure

($ billion)

Year	At current prices	At 1972 prices	Deductible advertising expenditure (50% of total– at 1972 prices)
1950	5.7	12.0	6.0
1951	6.4	12.9	6.5
1952	7.2	13.6	6.8
1953	7.8	14.0	7.0
1954	8.2	14.3	7.2
1955	9.2	15.6	7.8
1956	9.9	16.5	8.3
1957	10.3	16.6	8.3
1958	10.3	16.0	8.0
1959	11.3	17.1	8.6
1960	11.9	17.6	8.8
1961	11.8	17.1	8.6
1962	12.4	17.6	8.8
1963	13.1	18.3	9.2
1964	14.2	19.5	9.8
1965	15.3	20.6	10.3
1966	16.7	21.8	10.9
1967	16.9	21.4	10.7
1968	18.1	22.1	11.1
1969	19.5	22.6	11.3
1970	19.6	21.6	10.8
1971	20.7	21.6	10.8
1972	23.3	23.3	11.7
1973	25.1	24.0	12.0
1974	26.8	23.6	11.8
1975	28.2	22.9	11.5
1976	33.7	25.6	12.8
1977	38.1	27.0	13.5

Sources : U.S. Department of Commerce, Bureau of the Census, Statistical Abstract of the United States, 1978, p. 854. Historical Statistics of the United States, Colonial Times to 1970, p. 855. Economic Report of the President, U.S. Government Printing Office, Washington, D.C., 1979, p. 186. To convert advertising expenditure into 1972 prices, use has been made of the price index for services.

indirectly, to an increase in social welfare. A typical example of an intermediate service having enormous effects on private consumption is suggestive advertising, whose aim is to create an insatiable desire for new goods, thereby causing dissatisfaction with those already possessed. In contemporary consumer societies, a large part of advertising is suggestive and as such it eventually causes confusion and disorientation regarding the actual variety and properties of goods on the market. Thus, suggestive advertising ends up merely as a factor promoting price increases and a proliferation of largely similar marketed goods. On the other hand, informative advertising actually assists consumers to find their way out of the labyrinth of today's vast market.

In view of the above, 50 per cent of all expenditure on advertising, considered to correspond to the suggestive part of it, is deducted from private consumption. The amount deducted is shown in Table 3.

The assumption of 50 per cent is rather moderate and produces an upward bias of the EAW-index, for it rather disregards the enormous indirect impact of suggestive advertising, reflected in the overconsumption of several categories of virtually identical products and in the increasing wastefulness characterising affluent societies.

(c) Natural resources

The third and perhaps most important item that has to be deducted from private consumption is the real cost of accelerated exploitation of natural resources, resulting in their faster depletion.[6] Natural resources are usually classified as either exhaustible or reproducible. This traditional classification, however, is becoming increasingly vague and difficult to apply. A great many resources which were considered reproducible at the turn of the century, e.g. some species of the animal or vegetable kingdom, have ceased belonging in this class, since unconstrained utilisation has led to irreversible damage. Similarly to material capital, natural resources eventually become exhaustible if the rate of exploitation exceeds the rate of replacement over a period of time, the length of which is determined by the initial stock and the difference between these two rates. In the case of reproducible resources, the cost of using them enters into the calculation of the production cost of the national product at the prices determined in the market. The only problem is whether the market functions in such a way that the price corresponds to the marginal cost of production, i.e. whether it is a free competitive market.

By contrast, the marginal analysis used to evaluate exhaustible resources in the context of the competitive price mechanism, not only comes up against market imperfections, but also has to deal with problems of an intertemporal and intergenerational nature. The reason is that the evaluation concerns not a permanent flow of output from a renewable stock, but rather part of the exhaustible stock itself. Consequently, apart from the equilibrium conditions normally taken into account in flow markets, it is necessary that the equilibrium conditions applicable to stock markets be also satisfied.[7] What is even more important, however, is that, owing to the very exhaustibility of some resources, an evaluation requires the use of disequilibrium economics in order to take account of unanticipated discoveries of new deposits, unanticipated technological advances, shifts in oligopolistic or oligopsonistic forces, etc.

The question of developing a universally acceptable methodology for the evaluation of exhaustible natural resources is a perennial one. Pessimistic observations regarding the possibility of sustained growth in the absence of sufficient resources and especially in the face of an energy crisis, have drawn the attention of economists to the need for long term price restructuring and for re-evaluating the rates of exploitation of exhaustible resources.[8] Besides their theoretical and practical significance as to the desired rate and type of growth, these questions also have important policy implications regarding the "North-South" dialogue, since the developing countries' exports consist mainly of land-based (agricultural and mineral) products, while the structure of production in the advanced economies is more diversified.

The basic conclusion drawn from the economics of exhaustible resources is that, in a competitive market context, net prices — namely the price minus the marginal cost of extraction — will rise exponentially at a rate equal to the interest rate. On the other hand, under monopolistic conditions equilibrium can only be sustained if marginal revenue rises exponentially at a rate equal to the interest rate. Under oligopolistic conditions the price movements of natural resources are analogous to the competitive ones, depending on the specific market situation. With equally strong rival oligopolies, i.e. symmetrically placed oligopolistic firms, each taking the policy of the rest as given, we obtain Nash-equilibrium solutions. These solutions imply that long-run price movements are analogous to the competitive solutions and as the number of oligopolistic rivals increases the solutions approximate closer the competitive ones. With asymmetrically placed oligopolies where the branch is dominated by one or two big firms and there is also a relatively large number of small firms — the branch's competitive fringe — solutions are of the von Stackelberg type. The dominant firm's price policy will be such as to keep new entrants off the branch while making it unprofitable for the competitive fringe to use "backstop technology". This may have serious implications for technical progress and the introduction of substitutes.

With the occurrence of technological improvements in the extraction of resources the upward movement of prices due to the force of the interest rate may, for a time, be more than counterbalanced by the reduced (average and marginal) costs of extraction and prices might therefore fall for a time. But as extraction goes on, costs will turn up again and the rate of change of the resource price due to the force of the interest rate will be enhanced by the rate of change in the cost increase. Thus price may "exceed any pre-assigned value".[9] If there are no substitutes along the way, the resource price may increase continuously. This, of course, is not realistic to assume, since it is reasonable to expect that when its price exceeds a level $\bar{p}_1$ then, owing to "backstop technology", a perfect substitute for the resource becomes profitable to introduce. The price of the substitute $\bar{p}_2$ starts from the level where $\bar{p}_1 = \bar{p}_2$ and it will continue rising if cost-reducing technical progress is absent and the substitute is in scarce supply. When the price of the second substitute, in turn, exceeds a level $\bar{\bar{p}}_2$ then, owing to "backstop technology", a third substitute will become profitable to introduce, etc. In this way we obtain a leap-frog time path of resource substitution. It is clear, of course, that the rates of increase in the prices of substitute resources will be slower than the rates of increase in the price of the resource which is replaced. As the methodology used in drawing the above conclusions is based on partial equilibrium analysis, some doubts may be expressed regarding their validity. Precisely what does the interest rate represent and how is the equilibrium of capital markets affected when the resources market is not in equilibrium? Does the interest rate really correspond to the society's schedule of time preference, provided that markets are not perfectly competitive? Market disequilibria, instability and oligopolistic conditions cast doubt on the usefulness of the traditional analytical framework in investigating long term changes in the prices of exhaustible resources.

Perhaps the greatest difficulty in constructing a dynamic theoretical framework within which to evaluate exhaustible resources stems from intergenerational considerations. Thus, by using up exhaustible resources today, we are securing considerable benefits for ourselves, but at the same time we are passing great sacrifices on to the shoulders of future generations. These sacrifices consist in inhibiting future production from these resources and in forcing coming generations to pay higher extraction costs.

The intergenerational problem is not so much technical as normative. The present generation decides of its own volition what quantities will remain available to future generations. We can do something for or against future generations; they can do nothing for or against us. The problem may not be solved even if we assume the existence of perfect forward markets. The reason is that future generations cannot take part in the negotiations to determine the terms of exchange between present and future and the cost to be borne by them. W. D. Nordhaus recognises that current theory may be able to deal somewhat effectively with the problem of optimal distribution of productive resources in terms of efficiency, but it can do nothing about the normative problem of equality of enjoyment among generations or peoples.[10] A solution provided by R. Solow on this matter is based on the substitutability hypothesis between non-renewable resources and produced capital.[11] However, this approach cannot be considered wholly satisfactory, since substitution can only reach up to a certain point — fewer whales cannot be replaced by more machines. The least that the present generation can do is to bear the present value of future generations' sacrifices due to stock effects, i.e. pay for the benefits it enjoys and the sacrifices it passes on to the

shoulders of future generations. The present value of future
sacrifices due to using a resource now instead of postponing
its use is what Marshall and Keynes termed the "user cost"
of natural resources. This means that the price of non-
renewable resources used by the present generation should
include — in addition to marginal extraction cost and
interest — the costs passed on to future generations, i.e. the
marginal user cost of resources, which may be considered
a kind of compensation. The price should also include a
marginal loss of utility, owing to the damage suffered by
the environment in terms of natural beauty.

The latter two cost elements, i.e. user cost and the cost
due to environmental damage, could not be assessed, even
if perfect forward markets were in operation. Only government authorities could impose a lump-sum tax, which would
be an imputed outlay for these two cost components. Revenue from such taxation should then be invested, so that
the returns could be used to indemnify future generations
for the damage bequeathed to them.

Although there is some relationship between price movements and interest rates, empirical results have so far failed
to confirm some basic postulates of the economics of exhaustible resources. In fact, prices for the majority of natural
resources have moved at much lower levels than those predicted by theory.[12]

In the specific case of oil, the crisis which has beset
the world economy in recent years is likely to deepen. This
contingency will certainly materialise unless competitive
energy sources that can effectively replace oil in its various
uses are found and exploited. The market mechanism has
so far been unable to strike a balance between the opposing
forces underlying the crisis through the timely introduction
of truly representative prices.[13]

As a matter of fact, the prices of liquid fuels were so

low before 1973 that it became possible to support economic
growth in industrialised countries, which in turn has led to
the large-scale waste of the earth's energy resources. Typical
of the unwise energy policies pursued in the recent past is
the fact that, throughout the sixties, world oil consumption
was increasing at an average annual rate of 8 per cent.
Needless to say, the industrial nations bear a large share of
the responsibility for this unfortunate state of affairs.[14]

Regarding the rapid increase in oil prices since 1973,
a trend which seems likely to continue as long as efforts to
find suitable substitutes for known forms of energy remain
uncoordinated, it has to be admitted that mankind was
caught totally unprepared to face the new realities. The
world economy will therefore have to abide by OPEC's decisions and the energy crisis will persist, with destabilising
effects.

The energy crisis could have been averted if research
for oil substitutes had begun earlier. In that case, the prices
of oil substitutes would have been lower than what they are
now expected to be, owing to the technological improvements
and the economies of scale that would have been realised
in the meantime. Furthermore, the oil producing countries'
monopoly would have been weakened and they would have
been compelled to accept lower prices in order to retain part
of the market.

As regards other forms of energy (thermonuclear, solar,
aeolian, geothermal, etc.), which are unrelated to oil, it would
seem unlikely that they can solve mankind's energy problem
in the near future. This is because large scale research for
the discovery of new commercially exploitable energy sources
has begun fairly recently — certainly well after the outbreak
of the crisis. In connection with energy released by nuclear
fission, for instance, it is argued that "even if one large
thermonuclear power station is constructed daily, between

now and the year 2000, liquid fuels will account for more than 50 per cent of world demand for energy, should such demand continue to rise at an annual rate of 5 per cent".[15] These estimates were based on pre-1973 price and demand data for liquid fuels; of course, things have changed drastically since then. Nevertheless, irrespective of the actual level of future world demand for liquid fuels, the foregoing argument takes no account of the formidable hazard that radioactive waste represents for every form of life on this planet — a problem which science still seems unable to solve.[16]

Fewer problems, at least from the environmental point of view, seem to be connected with the production of energy by nuclear fusion, which leaves no radioactive waste. There are, however, daunting technical problems that will have to be tackled successfully before this method can become commercially exploitable — probably sometime over the next century.[17]

Even solar energy — possibly mankind's best chance to solve the energy problem — is not an easy or competitive solution, at least for the next fifteen to twenty years.[18]

Regardless of how long known energy resources are expected to last and of the difficulties involved in the wider use of nuclear or solar energy, there are many who believe that the problem of utilising the energy of the finite stock of terrestrial resources to further the economic development process goes much deeper. Reference is made here to the inexorable laws of nature, such as the entropy law, that seem to govern economic growth relying on a finite stock of energy.[19]

The effects of the law of entropy in relation to economic growth can perhaps best be understood if the world ecosystem is conceived as a closed system, in which one of the links is human economic activity. It can then be seen that the function of industrial development is to convert rapidly the valuable and finite stock of free terrestrial energy (low entropy) into bound energy (high entropy). Recycling cannot in the long run counterbalance the second law of thermodynamics, since use will again be made of free energy which will turn into bound energy. In the medium term though, and until more efficient techniques are developed, waste recycling could conceivably postpone the emergence of relevant problems, which are aggravated by the depletion of the finite stock of energy resources. If it were eventually possible for man to put to use other forms of energy flows (solar, aeolian, etc.), which by their nature are virtually unlimited, the entropy law would be practically irrelevant, since the economic process would occur as part of an open system.[20]

The energy crisis has become an extremely problem-ridden issue centring round the more or less imminent depletion of the world's petroleum deposits. Nevertheless, similar problems exist, *ceteris paribus,* with regard to other stock resources, such as metals, minerals, etc. It is natural then to express the hope that there is ahead of us an "age of substitutability", which will ease these formidable problems. In such an age "society will settle into a steady state of substitution and recycling".[21]

The foregoing discussion does not, of course, provide a method for assessing the effect of the exploitation of exhaustible resources on overall economic activity. It only indicates the adoption of approximate calculations, which are bound to involve a certain degree of arbitrariness.[22]

Recent research has shown that the rise in the prices of basic raw materials, including petroleum, has been much slower than the increase in labour cost.[23] It must therefore have been even slower than the increase expected in view of the conclusions drawn from theory (interest rate plus changes in cost). An explanation for this is that the rise in productivity due to technical progress has helped to keep down the prices of some exhaustible resources. This explanation rests on weak foundations, and would seem, at any rate, inadequate. A more reasonable explanation is that the market mechanism did not function in such a way as to take stock effects into account (user costs and scarcity rents) and shift them on to the shoulders of users in the form of higher prices. The problem of the appropriate market organisation for an optimal rate of resource use and depletion is very intricate. Expectations, rumours and risk-aversion attitudes play a very important role. In a competitive environment, e.g., if a rise in price of a natural resource is accompanied by rumours or expectations of a further rise in the future, resource owners will hold back supply while resource users will step up their efforts to invent and introduce substitutes. These attitudes will, in the long run, invalidate expectations because the increase in future supply and the introduction of substitutes will not call forth the expected price rise. If, on the other hand, an increase in price is considered to be temporary, then resource owners will try to dispose of their resources now while resource users will postpone resource purchases for tomorrow. This will ultimately lead to a downward pressure on prices. A monopolist of a natural resource, who is conscious of and willing to exercise his power, will tend to cut back supply now in anticipation of future price increases which are, in fact, engineered by his own behaviour. Ironically, a monopolistic market organisation tends to comply with the demands of the extreme conservationists more than a purely competitive market structure susceptible to rumours, expectations and risk-aversion.

TABLE 4

Expenditure on Specific Basic Raw Materials

($ billion)

Year	Actual expenditure at current prices (1)	Imputed expenditure at current prices* (2)	Difference (2)–(1)	Difference at 1972 prices
1950	6.8	6.8	—	—
1951	8.2	8.7	0.5	0.8
1952	8.1	8.2	0.1	0.2
1953	8.9	9.4	0.5	0.8
1954	8.6	10.0	1.4	2.2
1955	10.3	11.9	1.6	2.5
1956	11.5	13.6	2.1	3.2
1957	11.2	15.1	3.9	5.8
1958	9.4	14.3	4.9	7.1
1959	9.0	16.2	7.2	10.2
1960	9.1	17.8	8.7	12.1
1961	8.5	18.2	9.7	13.4
1962	8.7	20.4	11.7	15.9
1963	8.9	22.4	13.5	18.1
1964	9.6	25.4	15.8	20.9
1965	10.6	29.1	18.5	24.0
1966	12.0	34.3	22.3	28.1
1967	11.2	35.8	24.6	30.3
1968	11.7	40.4	28.7	33.9
1969	12.7	45.9	33.2	37.5
1970	13.2	50.5	37.3	40.3
1971	14.0	56.3	42.3	43.8
1972	15.9	65.9	50.0	50.0
1973	23.4	85.1	61.7	58.5
1974	56.6	103.0	46.4	39.7
1975	58.8	109.6	50.8	40.2
1976	68.9	134.5	65.6	49.3
1977	79.7	158.0	78.3	55.7

* Prices of raw materials have been inflated by 6% per year plus the annual rate of inflation in the U.S.A.

Sources: U.S. Department of Commerce, Bureau of the Census, Statistical Abstract of the United States 1961, 1978. IMF, International Financial Statistics Yearbook 1980. U.S. Department of the Interior, Bureau of Mines, Minerals Yearbook 1974, Vol. I. Figures have been deflated by the implicit deflator of private consumption.

In view of the above discussion, it can be argued that, owing to the oligopsonistic power of the advanced countries and the virtual absence of monopolistic consciousness of raw material supplying LDCs, prices of natural resources during the fifties and sixties and a part of the seventies were kept unduly low instead of rising by the long-term interest rate plus a premium for risk and user cost. For this reason, the prices of eight basic commodities (lead, copper, aluminium, zinc, gold, petroleum, iron and molybdenum) have been inflated by 6 per cent plus the yearly rate of inflation. The figure of 6 per cent is made up of two components: 3 per cent is the real riskless rate of interest. Several studies in the U.S.A., the U.K., Sweden etc. have shown the real interest rate to be 2-3 per cent in the absence of inflation. The remaining 3 per cent is an "educated guess" accounting for risk and user cost. For each year the cost of use of these materials is assessed as the difference between the imputed value of consumption (domestic production plus imports minus exports) — computed on the basis of the above assumptions concerning the theoretical price — and their current value as derived from market prices. The results of these estimates can be seen in Table 4.

(d) Rapid growth and the rising social cost of environmental pollution

This is an external cost, in the sense that costs related to the "use" of natural resources and borne by society are not usually imputed in private resource allocation decisions. The result is a divergence between the private and social costs involved in the production process. Since 1965, significant efforts have been made to control and prevent pollution in a wide variety of media. This implies that external diseconomies, which have generated social costs and therefore decreased social welfare, have been "internalised" to some extent in specific production functions. The "internalisation" of part of the social cost due to environmental degradation may lead to, among other things, an increase in the production of antipollution equipment and services, with a corresponding increase in conventionally measured GNP. Obviously, however, the value of these primarily corrective goods has to be deducted from the national income accounts.

The social costs of environmental pollution may be subdivided into "control costs" and "damage costs". Control costs comprise actual outlays aimed at preventing or correcting the destructive effects of pollution, while damage costs denote residual amounts of social cost owing to that part of environmental pollution not affected by control costs. Damages can be economic, cultural, aesthetic, psychological, etc. They include health damages associated with environmental pollution, the value of working time lost owing to environmentally linked incapacitation, the cost of aesthetic and environmental change, degradation, etc.

Damage costs are only potentially quantifiable costs whose magnitude affects both the level and the qualitative composition of social welfare. In this sense, damage costs are relatively more significant than control costs, not only because of their size, but also because they provide useful guideposts to policy makers for the coordination of efforts aimed at their minimisation. When for instance production-to-consumption externalities occur, the social marginal cost is higher than private marginal cost. Then the production plant causing pollution operates at a point other than that required to attain the social optimum, namely at a point where the private marginal cost of production equals the price of the product — or marginal revenue, if monopoly conditions prevail — disregarding social marginal cost. This happens precisely because part of production cost is external to polluters and is therefore borne by society and not by the firms themselves. If external cost could be internalised, by compelling the firms to pay damages to those harmed by the pollution resulting from their production, the level of their operation would surely be close to the social optimum. In the above sense, it is clear that the optimisation of the size of each and every plant does not lead to the attainment of a Paretian optimum for society as a whole, since this would disregard the highly important factor of external diseconomies.

What should be stressed, when the foregoing notions of marginal analysis are used, is that the "infinitesimal change" concept only applies so long as the economic system moves within certain limits — in the specific case, within a given scale of economic development. However, at advanced stages of affluence, increases in the social cost of environmental degradation may not be smooth and marginal, but are probably "catastrophic". Under such conditions, which are relevant to the level of economic development of concern to this essay, the equation of marginal utility or of private and social marginal cost would not be helpful in solving contemporary problems. This is so, because social cost would cease to increase marginally as the sequence lost its cohesion, in which case "the marginal cost of one more step may be to fall over the precipice".[24] Obviously, the postulates of marginalism do not apply in such cases. There are countless examples of the enormous divergence between private and social cost.[25]

In this essay, where the EAW-index is based on real private consumption, control cost has to be deducted so long as it serves to expand consumption. A case in point is when an individual is "forced" to buy a car incorporating a catalytic converter designed to cut down air pollution. It is impossible, however, to deduct from private consumption the amounts spent in connection with, say, the biological treatment of sewage. This is because it is technically impossible to ascertain whether and to what extent related investment expenditures are passed on to consumers, since what is measured is private consumption in real terms, and not at current prices.

The problem of estimation is different in the case of damage costs, where only approximate quantifications of the effective environmental destruction and degradation are possible. One could mention, for instance, the large losses — for present and future generations — caused by the destruction of vast expanses of forest land and the gradual spread of biological death in the earth's water resources. It therefore has to be emphasised that the cost of pollution — particularly damage cost as estimated in numerous studies — is but a fraction of the social cost due to ecological degradation.

It is also necessary to draw attention to the theoretical relationship between damage cost and control cost. They combine optimally at the point where marginal control cost equals marginal damage cost and the harm done by environmental degradation and therefore the total cost to society is minimised. Hence, from a theoretical standpoint, damage cost decreases as pollution control increases, a fact which would seem to suggest a diminishing rate of harmfulness of the remaining pollutants to society. Nevertheless, although from 1970 onwards damage cost due to air pollution showed signs of slowing down, overall damages were not drastically reduced.

One explanation — the easiest — is that the data are probably inadequate. Another and more likely explanation is that, depending on the kind of pollutants, there are longer or shorter time lags between the point where harmful substances are brought under control and the evidence of noxious effects on human health. To take an extreme example: the harmful effects of a radioactive leak which occurred for only an instant many years ago — theoretically even thousands of years ago — would still be with us today.

A third explanation is that science has not yet taken a definite stand concerning the limits beyond which each pollutant becomes harmful to health, agricultural production, heredity, etc. Thus, for instance, DDT was used almost without reservation during the fifties, whereas today it is regarded as a long term health hazard for both people and animals.

Hence, although control costs have been rising steeply since 1970, damage costs have remained at high levels. This might imply, *inter alia,* that today's "low" levels of pollutant emission are not really low enough to lead to a drastic curtailment of a number of diseases directly attributable to pollution. It may, in fact, be several years yet before scientists produce convincing proof of the exact degree of toxicity of the various substances polluting the environment. At any rate, the inverse relationship between control costs and damage costs is assumed only in the case of air pollution, for two reasons: first, because air pollution is related to reversible, short term illness and, second, because several researchers have argued that a 50 per cent reduction in the pre-1970 levels of air pollution maximises health benefits related to air quality.[26]

The foregoing discussion demonstrates that only a very small part of the effective damage caused by pollution and by the destruction of the environment in general can be assessed as damage cost. The enormous and unquantifiable social cost due to the deterioration of the quality of life is discussed in the next chapter, concerning quality-of-life indicators. Here it need only be said that the variables relating to environmental deterioration, which this essay attempts to "internalise" in the EAW-index, are most certainly underestimated. As a result, effective social costs remain largely external, being the most important factor underlying the degradation of the quality of life and of total social welfare in affluent societies.

The following is a detailed account of the methods employed in quantifying the social cost of air and water pollution and of solid wastes.

Air Pollution

Information on air pollution is more satisfactory than data on other pollution media, although there is a tendency to underestimate the levels of more recent years. Particularly as regards control cost, the annual Council on Environmental Quality (CEQ) reports put the figures for 1970 and 1975 at $1.8 billion and $11.6 billion respectively, with accompanying cumulative estimates for the ten-year periods 1971-1980 ($106.5 billion) and 1975-1984 ($175 billion). It is worth noting that the latest CEQ reports raise the estimate for the ten-year period 1978-1987 to $305.7 billion and the annual cost for 1978 to $19.3 billion.[27]

The above estimates were used to calculate the average annual growth rate of control cost for the intermediate years of the periods 1970-1975 and 1975-1978. Control cost data for air pollution at current and constant prices — conversion by means of the implicit deflator of private consumption — are given in Table 5.

The CEQ estimates of air pollution control cost comprise both private and public expenditures. Here also the problem is to find and deduct from private consumption the proportion of related expenditures directly affecting the size of this cost.

It is assumed that one half of all control cost is borne directly by private consumption in the form of increased demand for, say, domestic smoke eliminators, special filters

TABLE 5

Control Cost for Air Pollution

($ billion)

Year	At current prices	At 1972 prices
1970	1.8	1.9
1971	2.6	2.7
1972	3.8	3.8
1973	5.5	5.2
1974	8.0	6.8
1975	11.6	9.2
1976	13.7	10.3
1977	16.3	11.6

Source : Data for 1970, 1975 and 1978 are derived from the annual reports of the Council on Environmental Quality (CEQ). Trend values have been used for intermediate years.

for car exhaust fumes, etc. The other half is either borne by the public sector or is included in the production cost of manufacturing industry, which is required to construct special installations to cut down the emission of pollutants. Even where — depending on the degree of monopoly of each industrial branch — increased production cost is passed on to consumers by raising the final product prices, the calculations for the compilation of the EAW-index are not affected. This is so, because the starting point for all calculations is real private consumption.

Reference must also be made to various assumptions on which the residual, namely the damage cost due to air pollution, has been estimated. The base year for quantifying damage cost is 1970, as in the study by Ben-Chieh Liu and Eden Yu.[28] The calculations for that year were made for the 40 largest standard metropolitan statistical areas (SMSAs) while the coverage includes damage to human health, as well as soiling, material and crop damages. An extension of the results of the Liu-Yu survey to 148 SMSAs shows that

TABLE 6

Total Damages 1970

($ million)

1.	Health	2,720.4
2.	Soiling	5,033.0
3.	Material	38,419.8
4.	Crops	300.0
	Total	46,473.2

Source: B. Liu and E. Yu, *ibid.*

the damage cost of air pollution in 1970 totalled almost $46.5 billion (Table 6).

It is considered that this figure underestimates the actual situation because, at least as regards damage to human health, the calculations refer only to the original 40 SMSAs. However, since it is reasonable to assume that comparable conditions of air pollution prevail in most metropolitan areas of the United States, the damage cost due to the deterioration

TABLE 7

Damage Cost Due to Air Pollution

($ billion)

Year	At current prices	At 1972 prices	Year	At current prices	At 1972 prices
1950	11.5	20.2	1964	32.7	43.2
1951	13.5	22.3	1965	36.2	47.0
1952	14.4	23.3	1966	40.4	50.9
1953	15.4	24.4	1967	43.7	53.8
1954	15.7	24.7	1968	48.7	57.6
1955	17.4	27.1	1969	54.1	61.1
1956	18.6	28.4	1970	46.5	50.3
1957	19.9	29.4	1971	48.3	50.0
1958	20.5	29.7	1972	53.3	53.3
1959	22.6	32.1	1973	58.2	55.2
1960	23.9	33.3	1974	60.0	51.3
1961	25.3	34.8	1975	63.6	50.3
1962	27.8	37.8	1976	69.2	52.0
1963	29.9	40.0	1977	75.0	53.3

of human health must be considerably higher, raising the above estimated total accordingly.

The figure given by Liu and Yu for damage cost in 1970 provides a basis for the damage cost/GNP ratio calculated for the same year. Since data for individual years are not available, the same ratio was applied to the entire period under review, with annual deviations depending on actual levels of air pollution emissions as derived from CEQ reports. Owing to differences in the methods of calculating emissions before and after 1970, individual figures may not be fully comparable.[29] Estimates for damage cost due to air pollution during the period 1950-1977 are given in Table 7.

Water Pollution

With respect to water pollution, information on damage cost is unavailable. Data exist only for control cost. Thus, as in the case of control cost for air pollution, use was made of the Council of Environmental Quality (CEQ) data for the period 1970-1984, which give $6.1 billion for 1970 and $14.7 billion for 1975 (at current prices). For 1984, the corresponding figure is estimated to rise to $36.9 billion at 1975 prices.[30] For the period 1970-1977, the trend value of the above figures was used. As for the period prior to 1970, the ratio of water pollution control cost/GNP has been used as a starting point; this ratio was reduced according to the rate at which it changed between 1970 and 1975 (the water pollution control cost/GNP ratio increased from 0.6 in 1970 to 0.9 in 1975). Control cost data for water pollution, based on the preceding assumptions, are given in Table 8.

Since the fight against water pollution is mostly conducted by public authorities (federal, state or local), only a small part of this cost should be deducted from private consumption for the compilation of the EAW-index. However, in this case too, fully one half of control cost has been deducted, as no allowance was made for the remaining damages. Thus the probably overestimated part of control cost, regarded as being passed on to private consumption, must be largely

TABLE 8

Control Cost for Water Pollution

($ billion)

Year	At current prices	At 1972 prices	Year	At current prices	At 1972 prices
1950	0.9	1.6	1964	3.4	4.5
1951	1.0	1.6	1965	3.8	4.9
1952	1.1	1.8	1966	4.1	5.2
1953	1.2	1.9	1967	4.5	5.5
1954	1.3	2.0	1968	5.0	5.9
1955	1.5	2.3	1969	5.5	6.2
1956	1.6	2.4	1970	6.1	6.6
1957	1.7	2.5	1971	7.3	7.6
1958	1.9	2.7	1972	8.6	8.6
1959	2.1	3.0	1973	10.3	9.8
1960	2.3	3.2	1974	12.2	10.4
1961	2.5	3.5	1975	14.7	11.6
1962	2.8	3.8	1976	16.3	12.2
1963	3.1	4.1	1977	18.0	12.8

offset by the omitted damage cost due to water pollution, which should be deducted in full from private consumption were the relevant data available. To convert water pollution control cost from current into constant prices, use was made of the implicit deflator of private consumption.

Solid Waste Disposal

It is assumed that 95 per cent of solid waste is disposed of, so the remaining portion causes little or no damage. Cost data and CEQ estimates are available for the period starting with 1970.

Regarding the earlier years, the only available study covers the period 1963-1965.[31] This study provides data only for solid and not for liquid discharges and suggests a declining ratio of physical materials to dollar GNP. The rate of decline of material residuals during the longer period 1950-1970 was based on the 1963-1965 data. The foregoing assumption seems reasonable, considering that, to a large extent, the U.S. economy has turned into a service economy and there have been advances in technology, too. Consequently, the assumption of a 10 per cent drop in the

TABLE 9

Control Cost for Solid Waste Disposal

($ billion)

Year	At current prices	At 1972 prices	Year	At current prices	At 1972 prices
1950	1.2	2.0	1964	2.4	3.2
1951	1.3	2.1	1965	2.5	3.2
1952	1.3	2.1	1966	2.9	3.7
1953	1.4	2.2	1967	2.9	3.6
1954	1.3	2.1	1968	3.1	3.6
1955	1.4	2.2	1969	3.2	3.6
1956	1.6	2.4	1970	3.3	3.6
1957	1.8	2.7	1971	3.5	3.6
1958	1.7	2.4	1972	3.7	3.7
1959	1.8	2.6	1973	4.2	4.0
1960	1.9	2.6	1974	4.5	3.9
1961	2.0	2.8	1975	6.5	5.1
1962	2.1	2.9	1976	7.0	5.3
1963	2.2	3.0	1977	7.8	5.5

Source: Based on estimates in D. Plessas, "Social and Economic Welfare: Divergence and Turning Points", unpublished paper, 1979.

TABLE 10

Cost Due to Environmental Pollution
($ billion, at 1972 prices)

Year	Air Pollution		Water Pollution	Solid Wastes	Total Cost
	½ Control Cost	Damage Cost	½ Control Cost	Control Cost	
1950		20.2	0.8	2.0	23.0
1951		22.3	0.8	2.1	25.2
1952		23.3	0.9	2.1	26.3
1953		24.4	1.0	2.2	27.6
1954		24.7	1.0	2.1	27.8
1955		27.1	1.2	2.2	30.5
1956		28.4	1.2	2.4	32.0
1957		29.4	1.3	2.7	33.4
1958		29.7	1.4	2.4	33.5
1959		32.1	1.5	2.6	36.2
1960		33.3	1.6	2.6	37.5
1961		34.8	1.8	2.8	39.4
1962		37.8	1.9	2.9	42.6
1963		40.0	2.1	3.0	45.1
1964		43.2	2.3	3.2	48.7
1965		47.0	2.5	3.2	52.7
1966		50.9	2.6	3.7	57.2
1967		53.8	2.8	3.6	60.2
1968		57.6	3.0	3.6	64.2
1969		61.1	3.1	3.6	67.8
1970	1.0	50.3	3.3	3.6	58.2
1971	1.4	50.0	3.8	3.6	58.8
1972	1.9	53.3	4.3	3.7	63.2
1973	2.6	55.2	4.9	4.0	66.7
1974	3.4	51.3	5.2	3.9	63.8
1975	4.6	50.3	5.8	5.1	65.8
1976	5.2	52.0	6.1	5.3	68.6
1977	5.8	53.3	6.4	5.5	71.0

input-of-physical-materials to GNP ratio should be considered rather conservative. It is assumed that the full cost of solid waste disposal in agriculture, forestry, households, etc. is borne by private consumption. Hence, what should be deducted is 100 per cent of control cost for solid wastes.

The conversion of material disposal into abatement cost has been made on the assumption that the disposal of a ton of solid wastes cost $1.80 for the period 1950-1958, $2.0 for 1959-1960, $2.10 for 1961-1967, $2.20 for 1968-1972, $2.40 for 1973-1974 and from $3.55 in 1975 to $3.90 in 1980. Control cost data for this category are presented in Table 9. Consolidated data on the cost of environmental pollution, as used in the compilation of the EAW-index, are given in Table 10. Conversion of current into constant prices is again based on the implicit deflator of private consumption.

Apart from the three basic categories of pollutants, namely air and water pollutants and solid wastes, there are many other factors that systematically degrade the environment, such as noise, defective products, food poisoning, etc. Owing to insufficient data, however, they cannot be included in damage cost as factors conducive to a substantial diminution in the volume of "effective" consumption. This omission is one of the reasons why the calculated cost of pollution, a highly important determinant of social welfare, is a magnitude which systematically underestimates the true social cost of environmental deterioration.

(e) The cost of commuting

The use of transportation to and from the place of work and the related problem of traffic congestion are two of the worst aspects of urbanisation. The very existence of motor vehicles, mainly private cars, leads to a vicious circle. Traffic congestion is so complex a problem that it cannot be dealt with successfully even in New York or Los Angeles, where use is made of the latest and most sophisticated means of traffic control. Thus, despite continuous outlays for the construction of new infrastructure — not counting the social cost due to the loss of time, exhaust fumes, noise, traffic accidents, etc. — the problem of traffic congestion always remains steps ahead of any effort to solve it. As a result, an ever larger segment of the urban population moves away from city centres, into more or less remote suburbs, with a consequent emergence of yet another type of cost, commuting cost, over and above the already high social cost of urbanisation. To the extent that it can be quantified, transport cost includes the cost of fares, as well as the value of time wasted in travelling to and from the place of work. Here also there is a very considerable qualitative residual in addition to the measurable social cost of urbanisation, which is one of the parameters underlying the deterioration of the quality of life. Were it possible to quantify, even approximately, such social cost components as dissatisfaction with life in major urban centres or the fear caused by growing violence and crime, it would then be virtually certain that estimates would be considerably higher than the amount which is now included in the index of the economic aspects of welfare as the "social cost of urbanisation".

As was mentioned previously, the cost of commuting comes under the broader category of urbanisation cost and is estimated on the basis of, firstly, the direct cost of travel to and from the place of work by the various means of transport available and, secondly, the loss of time involved in travelling to and from work. The direct cost of travel comprises both the fares paid for the use of public means of conveyance and the expense involved in the use of private cars. Because of the lack of statistical data, it has been necessary to devise a valid method by which to estimate the number of people who made use of the various means of transport over the period 1950-1977.

According to a sample survey made in 1970, the highest proportion (77.7 per cent) of the working population travelled by private means, 8.9 per cent used public transport, and the remaining 13.4 per cent either worked at home or went to work on foot, by bicycle or by other means not involving a direct expense.[32] These percentages have been applied to total civilian employment for 1970 as given in the Economic Report of the President.[33] For those working at home or going to work on foot, it is assumed that their number (10,560 thousand in 1970) did not change between 1950 and 1977. They were mostly people living close to city centres, where the population increased over those years at very low rates compared with the number of people moving to the suburbs or to the outer periphery of urban centres.

To establish the time distribution between those workers who during the study period travelled by public transport and those who went to work by private car, the following assumptions have been made : First, according to data from the U.S. Statistical Abstract for 1977 (p. 645), the total number of people (not only workers) who used public transport showed a virtual decrease during the study period. The same rates of change have been applied to the total number of people who travelled to and from work using public conveyance (6,967 thousand, according to estimates based on the sample survey for 1970). Second, for the period 1950-1977, the working population has been adjusted by the (constant) number of people that went to work on foot and the number of those who commuted by public transport. The residual has given the number of people who commuted by private car. To determine further the cost of commuting by private car, it has been necessary to establish

TABLE 11

Ways of Commuting to and from Place of Work
(In thousands of individuals)

Year	Pedestrians etc.	Commuting by public transport	Commuting by private car	(Number of cars)	Total civilian employment
1950	10,560	16,386	31,972	(27,141)	58,918
1951	10,560	15,107	34,294	(29,112)	59,961
1952	10,560	13,929	35,761	(30,357)	60,250
1953	10,560	12,843	37,776	(32,068)	61,179
1954	10,560	11,842	37,707	(32,009)	60,109
1955	10,560	10,959	40,651	(34,508)	62,170
1956	10,560	10,521	42,718	(36,263)	63,799
1957	10,560	10,100	43,411	(36,851)	64,071
1958	10,560	9,696	42,780	(36,316)	63,036
1959	10,560	9,308	44,762	(37,998)	64,630
1960	10,560	8,925	46,293	(39,298)	65,778
1961	10,560	8,701	46,485	(39,461)	65,746
1962	10,560	8,484	47,658	(40,456)	66,702
1963	10,560	8,272	48,930	(41,536)	67,762
1964	10,560	8,065	50,680	(43,022)	69,305
1965	10,560	7,845	52,683	(44,722)	71,088
1966	10,560	7,657	54,678	(46,416)	72,895
1967	10,560	7,472	56,340	(47,826)	74,372
1968	10,560	7,292	58,068	(49,293)	75,920
1969	10,560	7,118	60,224	(51,124)	77,902
1970	10,560	6,967	61,100	(51,867)	78,627
1971	10,560	6,550	62,010	(52,640)	79,120
1972	10,560	6,242	64,900	(55,093)	81,702
1973	10,560	6,326	67,523	(57,320)	84,409
1974	10,560	6,590	68,785	(58,391)	85,935
1975	10,560	6,626	67,597	(57,382)	84,783
1976	10,560	6,730	70,195	(59,588)	87,485
1977	10,560	7,239	72,747	(61,754)	90,546

Data processed from the following sources : U.S. Department of Commerce, Bureau of the Census, Statistical Abstract of the United States, 1977, pp. 644 and 645. Economic Report of the President, U.S. Government Printing Office, Washington, D.C., 1979, p. 216.

the number of vehicles used. This has been calculated on the assumption that the 1970 car/passengers ratio remained unchanged throughout the period under consideration.[34] The number of commuters by transport category and the number of cars used are shown in Table 11. Estimates for inter-mediate years, for which data are unavailable, are based on trend figures.

The total cost of commuting between home and the place of work has been calculated, as mentioned earlier, on the basis of direct travel cost and the value of time spent. Direct travel cost is further broken down into public trans-port fares and cost of travel by private vehicle. To estimate fares, the figure for public transport users (Table 11) has been multiplied by 250 days at 60 cents a day to obtain the annual totals given in Table 12.[35] For people commuting by private vehicle, travel cost has been taken to be one third of the annual cost of car upkeep, including repairs, insurance premiums, fuel, etc. However, the annual depreciation of private cars has been omitted, since it is included in the value of services from consumer durables.

It was estimated that the average annual cost of running a private car in 1972, excluding depreciation, totalled about $960.[36] One third of this sum ($320) is assumed to cover the cost of travel to and from work. This seems to be a realistic assumption, since the average distance between home and workplace is put at roughly nine miles. So, a round trip of eighteen miles, multiplied by the number of working days, gives roughly one third of a private car's average annual mileage. The amount of $320, assumed to be the average annual cost of travelling to work and back by private car in 1972, changed over the years half as much as the time required to get to work and return home. The figures derived by multiplying the number of private vehicles in use for commuting by the esti-mated annual cost are given in Table 12 (second column).

TABLE 12

Cost of Commuting to and from Place of Work

($ billion, at 1972 prices)

Year	Expenditure for commuting by public transport	Expenditure for commuting by private car	Cost from the loss of time	Total cost
1950	2.5	5.5	0.8	8.8
1951	2.3	6.0	1.7	10.0
1952	2.1	6.4	2.6	11.1
1953	1.9	7.0	3.6	12.5
1954	1.8	7.1	4.5	13.4
1955	1.6	7.9	6.1	15.6
1956	1.6	8.4	7.9	17.9
1957	1.5	8.8	9.5	19.8
1958	1.5	8.9	10.9	21.3
1959	1.4	9.5	12.9	23.8
1960	1.3	10.0	15.0	26.3
1961	1.3	10.3	16.7	28.3
1962	1.3	10.8	19.0	31.1
1963	1.2	11.3	21.2	33.7
1964	1.2	11.9	23.9	37.0
1965	1.2	12.6	26.9	40.7
1966	1.1	13.3	29.9	44.3
1967	1.1	14.0	33.1	48.2
1968	1.1	14.7	36.6	52.4
1969	1.1	15.5	40.5	57.1
1970	1.0	16.0	43.7	60.7
1971	1.0	16.6	47.3	64.9
1972	0.9	17.6	53.1	71.6
1973	0.9	18.7	58.1	77.7
1974	1.0	19.3	59.9	80.2
1975	1.0	19.3	60.7	81.0
1976	1.0	20.4	66.5	87.9
1977	1.1	21.4	72.9	95.4

Data processed from the following sources: U.S. Department of Commerce, Bureau of the Census, Statistical Abstract of the United States, 1973 and 1977. Economic Report of the President, U.S. Government Printing Office, Washington, D.C., 1979.

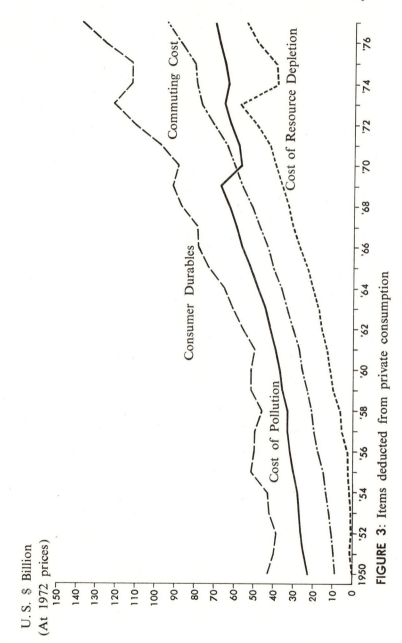

FIGURE 3: Items deducted from private consumption

The foregoing assumptions concern the calculation of the direct cost of commuting.

The second determinant of the cost of commuting is the indirect cost of time spent travelling between home and workplace. According to available data, the time taken to get to work and back in 1965-1966 was 52 minutes for men and 42 minutes for women.[37] For the period between 1965-1966 and 1977, it is assumed that the length of the round trip increased by 2 minutes a year. This takes account of worse traffic conditions in downtown districts, owing to the growing number of people living at ever greater distances from metropolitan areas. For the period before 1965-1966, 2 minutes a year have been deducted from commuting time. A time loss of up to twenty minutes a day is not reckoned as a cost item in the calculations. The length of time lost in excess of twenty minutes has been multiplied by the number of commuters, and the product by the number of working days. The final result, representing hours lost each year in travelling to and from work, has been multiplied by the real average hourly wage rate (use has again been made of the implicit deflator of private consumption). The cost of time spent in commuting is shown in Table 12 (third column). The total cost of commuting (cost of time spent plus direct cost of travel) is presented in the last column of the same table.[38]

(f) Private health and education outlays of an investment or corrective nature

Since private consumption has been assumed to be the starting-point for the compilation of the EAW-index, its components should be closely correlated to social welfare. However, while health expenses for instance have increased faster than private consumption, relevant indicators suggest that there has been little improvement in public health. The implication may be that, beyond a certain point, health expenses are not correlated to improvements in the quality of the final product "health". This means that not all expenses in connection with health should be regarded as consumer spending.[39] In fact, although health outlays in the United States account for one of the highest percentages of GNP, health conditions are not the best in the world. For instance, there are several other countries where average life expectancy at birth is higher or where infant mortality rates are lower.[40] In this respect, the United States shows a slow improvement, despite enormous outlays. It is therefore quite likely that the beneficial effects of health expenditure over the last two or three decades have been largely offset by adverse factors, regardless of whether public health expenditure is an investment in human capital or merely a consumer outlay. Some of these adverse factors are environmental pollution, the mental stress inherent in today's way of life, the uneven distribution of health services among the various population groups, and so on.[41]

Hence, it seems that a large portion of the increase in health outlays is in the nature of corrective spending owing to peculiarities of the industrialised way of life. Accordingly, corrective health expenditure, namely expenditure intended to remedy harm caused to human health by the conditions of life in today's rich economies, must be omitted from the EAW-index.[42]

It has thus been deemed appropriate to deduct from private consumption 50 per cent of the annual increment in per capita health outlays (at constant prices) during the study period. The remaining 50 per cent is regarded as an improvement in the overall level of health services supplied, as shown in Table 13. The base year for these calculations is 1950, for which it is assumed that no part of health expenditure was corrective. Consequently, private health out-

TABLE 13

Private Expenditure on Health

($ billion)

Year	Expenditure at current prices	Expenditure at 1972 prices	Estimated expenditure based on population growth and an improvement rate, at 1972 prices	Waste at 1972 prices
1950	9.2	22.7	22.7	—
1951	9.8	23.1	23.1	—
1952	10.6	23.7	23.6	0.1
1953	11.4	24.6	24.3	0.3
1954	12.4	25.9	25.1	0.8
1955	13.2	27.0	25.9	1.1
1956	14.3	28.2	26.7	1.5
1957	15.6	29.6	27.6	2.0
1958	16.9	30.6	28.3	2.3
1959	18.6	32.2	29.3	2.9
1960	21.3	35.7	31.3	4.4
1961	22.8	37.1	32.2	4.9
1962	25.3	40.2	34.0	6.2
1963	27.2	42.1	35.2	6.9
1964	30.5	46.3	37.5	8.8
1965	32.7	48.4	38.8	9.6
1966	35.8	50.8	40.3	10.5
1967	39.3	52.1	41.1	11.0
1968	44.4	55.4	43.1	12.3
1969	51.3	59.9	45.6	14.3
1970	58.1	63.8	47.8	16.0
1971	64.7	66.8	49.5	17.3
1972	72.9	72.9	52.8	20.1
1973	81.7	78.6	55.8	22.8
1974	92.7	81.6	57.5	24.1
1975	108.3	85.1	59.5	25.6
1976	126.2	90.5	62.5	28.0
1977	142.3	93.1	64.0	29.1

Sources : OECD, National Accounts of OECD Countries, 1960-1977, vol. II, p. 22. Historical Statistics of the United States, Colonial Times to 1970, p. 74. U.S. Department of Commerce, Bureau of the Census, Statistical Abstract 1978. Private expenditure on health has been deflated by the sub-index for "medical care" of the consumer price index.

lays must have led to a direct improvement in public health, since it seems reasonable to accept that at that time the side-effects of economic growth on health were limited.

Similar problems arise in connection with expenditure on education. Here also the question is what proportion of total outlays is essential for maintaining the "quality" of the stock of human capital, without which it would be impossible for a highly specialised industrial economy to keep on functioning and advancing satisfactorily. In other words, it is a question of what proportion of outlays on education is in the nature of investment and must therefore be deducted from private consumption.[43]

In this vein, a reasonable assumption would be to consider primary and secondary education essential for maintaining the skills of "human capital". As regards higher education, however, the widespread notion that it is the best possible form of investment for young men and women seems generally exaggerated. In fact, this notion is not entirely in keeping with reality, at least as far as the financial yield of investment in education is concerned.[44] Beyond any improvement in the income level of college and university graduates, the aspects of a person's life which seem to be radically differentiated by higher education are vocational success and the gaining of a different and deeper insight into personal and family problems, as well as into social issues. It is seen, for instance, that the "educational level" is negatively correlated with the number of jobless as a percentage of the total number of employed persons, as well as with the percentage of people who lost their job once or those who change their job often, etc. By contrast, college and university graduates enjoy a longer annual leave and have better prospects of promotion than other people.[45] This suggests that a considerable part of education is a "consumer" good, at least with respect to the higher educational levels, so that it directly increases total personal welfare and is not confined merely to raising productivity, as in the case of wage and salary differentiations.[46] This argument is corroborated by the fact that, when somebody decides to take a college or university course, this decision expresses the free will of a responsible adult. In other words, the person concerned chooses to "consume" higher education according to the "consumer sovereignty" he is supposed to command.[47]

For the calculations, it is assumed that investment outlays, which are deductible from private consumption, comprise private expenditure on primary and secondary education plus half of private spending on higher education. Although with regard to private expenditure on higher education it is certainly arbitrary to distinguish between investment and consumption on a fifty-fifty basis, it has been deemed acceptable for lack of a more appropriate method. The other half of higher education expenditure is supposed to enhance personal well-being. Pertinent figures are given in Table 14.

TABLE 14

Private Expenditure on Education

($ billion)

Year	At current prices	At 1972 prices	Expenditure on primary, secondary and half of higher education at 1972 prices
1950	1.6	3.7	2.7
1951	1.7	3.8	2.7
1952	1.9	3.8	2.7
1953	2.0	3.9	2.8
1954	2.1	4.2	3.0
1955	2.3	4.6	3.3
1956	2.6	4.7	3.4
1957	2.8	4.8	3.5
1958	3.1	5.4	3.9
1959	3.4	5.6	4.0
1960	4.2	6.7	4.8
1961	4.5	7.1	5.1
1962	4.9	7.6	5.5
1963	5.4	8.1	5.8
1964	5.9	8.7	5.9
1965	6.7	9.5	6.5
1966	7.7	10.5	7.1
1967	8.5	11.1	7.5
1968	9.8	12.2	8.3
1969	10.9	12.9	8.8
1970	12.3	13.6	9.2
1971	13.5	14.2	9.7
1972	14.8	14.8	10.1
1973	16.2	15.2	10.3
1974	17.7	14.7	10.0
1975	19.6	14.9	10.1
1976	21.6	15.4	10.5
1977	23.7	15.7	10.7

Sources : OECD, National Accounts of OECD Countries, 1960-1977, vol. II, pp. 22-23. Historical Statistics of the United States, Colonial Times to 1970, p. 317. U.S. Department of Commerce, Bureau of the Census, Statistical Abstract 1978, p. 135. U.N., Yearbook of National Accounts Statistics, 1967, pp. 722-23. Use has been made of the implicit deflator of education expenditure.

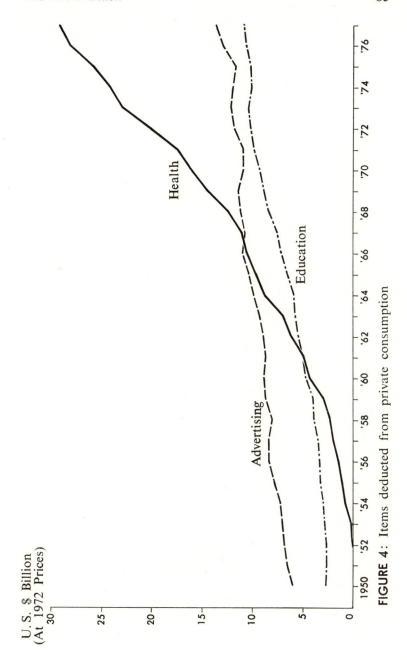

FIGURE 4: Items deducted from private consumption

2. Items Added to Private Consumption in the Construction of the EAW-Index

(a) Services from the stock of public capital

Public capital is considered to include such items as hospitals, schools, museums, etc. These are collectively consumed goods, that is, goods that can be used indivisibly — except in the case of natural restrictions — by all the members of a community. Radio and television broadcasts are another example of a public good, the services of which can be "consumed" collectively.

By contrast, private goods are governed by the principle of divisibility or personal consumption, which precludes the consumption of a specific quantity of the good by more than one person at one and the same time.

Obviously, the services supplied by public capital are of tremendous importance for the promotion of social welfare. The imputed annual costs of these services must therefore be taken into account in the EAW-index. To calculate the value of services from public fixed capital, use has been made of the flow of funds accounts of the Federal Reserve Board, relating to capital consumption. U.S. Congress estimates give the stock of public buildings (except dwellings owned by federal or state authorities) for the period 1952-1968. On the basis of these figures and related data, the value of the stock of public buildings has been estimated for the remaining years of the study period. It has been assumed that only 50 per cent of public buildings supply services enhancing social welfare, while the other 50 per cent comprises buildings that either do not contribute directly to social welfare (e.g. penitentiaries) or participate in the production process (e.g. factories) and only indirectly affect income and consumption. Thus, the annual flow of services has been calculated for half of the existing public buildings, using the average long term interest rate in the private sector.

TABLE 15

Imputed Value of Services of Public Buildings that Contribute to an Increase in Economic Welfare

(At 1972 prices)

Year	$ billion	Year	$ billion	Year	$ billion
1950	7.5	1960	11.5	1970	17.5
1951	7.8	1961	12.0	1971	18.2
1952	8.1	1962	12.6	1972	18.9
1953	8.4	1963	13.0	1973	19.7
1954	8.8	1964	13.8	1974	20.5
1955	9.1	1965	14.5	1975	21.3
1956	9.5	1966	15.1	1976	22.1
1957	10.0	1967	15.6	1977	23.0
1958	10.5	1968	16.2		
1959	11.0	1969	16.8		

Data processed from the following sources : Historical Statistics of the United States, Colonial Times to 1970. U.S. Department of Commerce, Bureau of the Census, Statistical Abstract 1975 and 1978. Estimates for the years for which no data are available.

(b) Services from durable consumer goods

Outlays for the acquisition of consumer durables have been deducted from private consumption because, similarly to investment spending, they do not contribute directly to personal well-being. The services derived from these goods do, however, contribute to personal welfare and are therefore added as annual flows to the EAW-index, just as in the case of services from public capital.

Here it should be noted that most consumer durables are subject to technological obsolescence, which forces them out of use before they actually become useless. This is why the total of all the annual services supplied by such goods — as calculated in the index — is less than 100 per cent of their initial value. The difference corresponds to the value of services not used, precisely because of the technological obsolescence of the respective goods.

Among the innumerable examples of consumer durables subject to rapid obsolescence owing to technological advances is the motor car. It has been estimated that the annual cost of changing models reaches as high as 25 per cent of output value and was roughly $10 billion in 1972. This cost is always charged to the consumer because, even if someone prefers an old model that is cheaper by the cost of innovations, he cannot find it after a certain length of time which is much shorter than the useful life span of the car.

It could perhaps be mentioned that, far from being confined to the class of consumer durables, this phenomenon is so widespread as to be typical of the wastefulness and overconsumption that are prevalent in industrial societies and serve to worsen income inequalities between rich and poor countries. For instance, it is estimated that the quantity of grain used in rich countries as animal feed is much more than the amount consumed in poor countries to feed their human population. It is also estimated that 65 per cent of the food served in U.S. restaurants ends up in the garbage can, while the corresponding percentage for middle-income households is as high as 25 per cent. In this way, while "the poor world is suffering from the deprivation caused by too little, the rich world is increasingly suffering from the problems caused by too much".[48]

To estimate the annual value of services from consumer durables (Table 16), the first step was to evaluate the existing capital stock. The base year chosen is 1940, on the assumption that previous investment in such durable goods had for the most part been fully depreciated by 1950, the first year to which the EAW-index calculations refer. The measurements are based on a breakdown of expenditures on durable goods, such as household equipment, motor cars, etc., at 1972 prices. Regarding household equipment (furniture, appliances, etc.), it has been assumed that 60 per cent consists of goods that supplied the same or similar services in the past. The remaining 40 per cent comprises technologically advanced products (e.g. dishwashers, vacuum cleaners), which now do a large part of the job formerly done by the housewife and increase social welfare accordingly, to the extent that they help to liberate women from some of their conventional duties. However, the services of these goods, which should be incorporated in the EAW-index, are

TABLE 16

Imputed Value of Services from Consumer Durables

($ billion, at 1972 prices)

Year	Motor cars	Furniture etc.	Total	Year	Motor cars	Furniture etc.	Total
1950	9.2	4.0	13.2	1964	21.2	10.8	32.0
1951	10.4	4.5	14.9	1965	22.6	11.3	33.9
1952	11.4	5.0	16.4	1966	24.0	11.8	35.8
1953	12.7	5.5	18.2	1967	25.0	12.4	37.4
1954	13.7	6.0	19.7	1968	26.8	12.9	39.7
1955	15.9	6.6	22.5	1969	28.4	13.6	42.0
1956	16.7	7.2	23.9	1970	28.8	14.2	43.0
1957	17.4	7.8	25.2	1971	30.3	14.9	45.2
1958	17.8	8.4	26.2	1972	32.6	15.7	48.3
1959	17.8	9.0	26.8	1973	35.0	16.7	51.7
1960	17.8	9.3	27.1	1974	35.5	17.7	53.2
1961	18.0	9.5	27.5	1975	37.6	18.6	56.2
1962	18.9	9.8	28.7	1976	39.0	19.6	58.6
1963	19.4	10.2	29.6	1977	41.4	20.7	62.1

Source: Estimates based on data of the U.S. Department of Commerce, Bureau of Economic Analysis, Survey of Current Business, January 1976 and July 1978.

not taken into account. This is because it is assumed that their value is counterbalanced by an equally deductible sum, namely by that part of the annual imputed value of household services — one of the major "plus" items of the EAW-index — which now corresponds to the market value of the services of household appliances.

Regarding now the 60 per cent of household equipment whose services are added to private consumption in the compilation of the EAW-index, an average normal life span of twenty years has been assumed. This is the case mainly of services from furniture and other household appliances, which are spread equally over a period of twenty years after acquisition.[49] As far as motor cars are concerned, it has been assumed that their true technological life span is around fifteen years, but that they are mostly scrapped in ten years owing to technological obsolescence. It is further assumed that the services they supply are greater in the initial years and gradually decrease. Thus, 15 per cent of the value remaining each year is depreciated. This means that roughly 80 per cent of the car's initial value is used up as annual services by the end of ten years, leaving 20 per cent as scrap value.[50]

(c) Household services

This is one of the items significantly affecting economic welfare. Whether or not housework is supplied and paid for through market channels depends largely on the phase of economic development in which a given society finds itself. In the past, most of this work was done by housewives as a non market activity and thus did not appear in the national accounts. Today, a large part of it is carried out with the help of electrical appliances whose value is recorded by the market. Also, a considerable part of the services supplied by the housewife within her home has nowadays taken the form of market transactions; for example, daily meals at self-service restaurants, clothes washing at laundries or cleaners, and so on. At the same time, growing numbers of women are cutting down on housework to become part of the labour force. Besides misrepresenting the actual size of consumption in industrial societies, the omission of the value of housework from the national accounts imparts an upward bias to the more recent observations of the time series in comparison with the past, to the extent that some of the non market services of previous periods now go through the market mechanism. Consequently, to render data comparable over the years, it is necessary to estimate the value of housework over time.

The imputed value of housework has been quantified in the EAW-index on the assumption that, for the average household, the required amount of housework — whether supplied within or outside the market — is equivalent to the employment of one person for five hours a day for 365 days a year.[51] It has also been assumed that non market housework is "paid" for at the real average wage rate in the private urban sector.[52] Thus, by calculating the total number of hours of work per unit of time and the value of housework per unit of time, it has been possible to estimate the imputed value of non remunerated housework in the EAW-index. The resulting figures are shown in Table 17.

In the compilation of the EAW-index, the total annual number of hours of non remunerated housework was reduced over time in accordance with the services supplied by laundries, cleaners, self-service restaurants, etc. and by the services supplied by paid domestics.[53] The hours of unpaid housework should be reduced further, owing to the constantly increasing use of various household appliances, which represent about 40 per cent of household equipment.

TABLE 17

Imputed Value of Household Services

(At 1972 prices)

Year	$ billion	Year	$ billion	Year	$ billion
1950	143.4	1960	215.2	1970	270.1
1951	146.5	1961	220.8	1971	278.0
1952	153.5	1962	229.2	1972	290.9
1953	163.9	1963	234.3	1973	290.0
1954	170.1	1964	241.7	1974	271.9
1955	179.9	1965	249.3	1975	264.4
1956	189.8	1966	253.9	1976	261.6
1957	195.9	1967	266.4	1977	260.7
1958	199.7	1968	266.1		
1959	208.5	1969	269.8		

Data processed from the following sources : Economic Report of the President, U.S. Government Printing Office, Washington, D.C., 1979. U.S. Department of Commerce, Bureau of the Census, Statistical Abstract 1978.

However, since annual service flows have not been estimated for these goods, no deduction has been made for the amount of housework saved as a result of their use, on the assumption that the two magnitudes are mutually offset, as mentioned in the section on durable goods.

(d) Leisure time

From the standpoint of social welfare, it is very important to know how far economic growth has led to an increase in leisure time. The question to ask is whether and to what extent the productivity gain accompanying economic growth translates into material output or leisure. It would appear, contrary to what one would expect, that the economic growth model followed by industrial nations is clearly in favour of increasing product growth, while the rate of increase in leisure time seems to be much lower.[54] Thus, over the period 1950-1977, per capita product increased by about 75 per cent, while weekly hours of work fell by only 9.5 per cent (from 39.8 in 1950 to 36 in 1977).

The introduction of leisure time as a scarce good in the analysis of economic phenomena may better explain the diminishing or even negative marginal utility of income beyond a certain level of economic growth.[55] This is because, at relatively higher income levels, it is reasonable to assume that a large part of basic human wants has been satisfied. It seems very likely, however, that the diminishing marginal utility of income at those levels is also due to the lack of sufficient time to make use of an ever growing number of consumer goods.

The diminishing marginal utility of income, together with the postulated positive income effect regarding the demand for leisure time at high income levels, should lead to a continuous increase in demand for leisure in affluent societies.[56] That this does not seem to be the case, at least in the United States during the study period, when increases in leisure time were fairly slow, must then be attributed to the prevalence of the substitution effect. Of course, this is contrary to conventional theory, according to which the income effect must have relatively greater force with respect to a presumed luxury good such as leisure time. Predominance of the substitution effect implies, however, that the supply of labour increases with the rise in its price, while demand for leisure time drops or remains unchanged. Such behaviour may be regarded as the result of the involvement of the individual members of a consumer society in acute positional competition. In this respect, what seems to be important is not the absolute but the relative income position of individuals. Consequently, if they are to maintain or improve their relative position, the individuals involved in positional competition — whose numbers are increasing *pari passu* with economic growth — are "forced" to work longer hours. It is only by doing so that they are able to afford the positional goods that will enable them to rise on the social scale.[57]

It was originally believed that economic growth would eventually shorten working time. This belief has not been confirmed in today's advanced economies. The implication is that mankind is constantly being driven farther away from the point of long term equilibrium, where it could sit back and enjoy the fruits of civilisation in peace and quiet. The reason is that the growth of the physical product, in the way it takes place in modern economies, is a source of constant stress and compels people to work harder in order to be able to afford the unending stream of "new" goods being supplied by the system.

In estimating the value of free time, it has to be decided whether leisure is a final good or whether it is one of the several consumer products that make up the final good "recreation". In the former case productivity gains over time do not have to be taken into account, while in the latter technological progress must be considered.[58] In this essay, leisure has been quantified according to the first notion, namely that it is a final good regardless of productivity gains. This approach is based on the assumption that, nowadays, even if someone has more means for taking advantage of free time, there might be other factors with the opposite effect, such as the feeling of stress that seems to be present even during our hours of leisure. For instance, does driving a motor car increase the pleasure that an hour's free time offers to its owner? It would be reasonable to assume that, in the early years of its existence, the motor car did indeed contribute a great deal to the enjoyment of free time. There are doubts, however, whether younger generations of car users gain as much satisfaction. Various problems have cropped up in the meantime, which have turned what was originally a highly enjoyable experience into a source of deep displeasure.

In the present context, leisure has been quantified on the basis of, first, the amount of free time available to various segments of the population (workers, non-workers, etc.), second, the size of each population segment and third, the estimated value of leisure time (at 1972 prices).

For the first of the above items and for the period prior to 1965, leisure data from a sample survey by Robinson and Converse suggest that there has been no change in the amount of free time available to the four major population segments, namely male workers, male non-workers, female workers and female non-workers.[59] This conclusion coincides with the findings of a 1954 survey, which have been used by Tobin and Nordhaus.[60]

For the second item, the size of each population segment has been estimated on the basis of annual U.S. labour force statistics.

Lastly, for the third item, namely the value of leisure time, use has been made of half of the average nominal hourly wage rate in the urban sector of the U.S. economy in 1972, since it is assumed that leisure does not involve a productivity gain.

In contrast to the data covering the years until 1965, which show no significant change in leisure time, a sample survey for the period 1965-1975 suggests a substantial change in comparison with the previous trend.[61] It has been found that total hours of leisure for the various population categories rose from 34.8 a week in 1965 to 38.5 a week in 1975. Since the sample was very small, it must be attempted to determine whether the conclusions from the 1965-1975 survey may be considered representative of overall trends in the relationship between working time and leisure in U.S.

society. In this respect, the following possibilities have been investigated :

First, whether weekly hours of work in the U.S. economy have decreased, and in which sectors.

Second, whether the number of part-time workers increased during the study period.

Third, whether the participation of women in total employment has increased, and by how much.

The answer to the first question is that, over the entire study period, the number of working hours remained virtually unchanged at the level of 40 hours a week in manufacturing and 37.5 in construction, while it dropped drastically in the service sector. This had the effect of lowering the weekly total of working hours from 39.8 in 1950 to 36.0 in 1977 throughout the private (non agricultural) sector of the U.S. economy.[62] Needless to say, these developments are directly associated with the conditions generally affecting labour mobility, especially over the past ten years.

The answer to the second question is that the number of part-time workers rose from 8.5 million in 1965 to 14.5 million in 1977.[63] The assumption that part-time workers are mainly employed in the service sector is corroborated by available data, which suggest a drop in weekly hours of work in that sector.

Additional support to this view is provided by the answer to the third question, which is that the participation of female workers in total employment increased from 29.4 per cent in 1950 to 40.5 per cent in 1977. In absolute figures, this increase is equivalent to 19 million more employed women in 1977.[64]

From these developments it can be inferred that, during the period 1950-1977 (or 1950-1975 when more recent data are not available), there was no substantial decline in working time, apart from some apparent reductions in services and trade, where the participation of part-time — mainly female — workers is fairly high.

This inference coincides with the findings of the 1975 sample survey, according to which the weekly hours of "paid" work of the whole sample remained virtually unchanged over the period 1965-1975 (actually, they dropped from 33 hours a week in 1965 to 32.5 in 1975).[65] According to the same survey, the increase in leisure time is mainly attributable to a decrease in hours devoted to family care from 25.4 a week in 1965 to 20.5 a week in 1975.[66] Thus, if the hypothesis made in the Robinson survey is accepted, the imputed value of housework over the same period will have to be reduced commensurately.

As was mentioned previously, it has been assumed that those engaged in market activities similar to housework have five times higher productivity than those engaged in non-

TABLE 18

Imputed Value of Leisure Time

(At 1972 prices)

Year	$ billion	Year	$ billion	Year	$ billion
1950	368.4	1960	412.9	1970	485.6
1951	371.5	1961	419.3	1971	493.9
1952	376.1	1962	425.2	1972	507.2
1953	378.5	1963	433.7	1973	517.9
1954	385.9	1964	442.4	1974	524.6
1955	387.0	1965	451.2	1975	526.9
1956	390.1	1966	458.0	1976	538.0
1957	396.2	1967	463.6	1977	547.2
1958	402.9	1968	472.1		
1959	408.3	1969	480.0		

Data processed from the following sources: Economic Report of the President, U.S. Government Printing Office, Washington, D.C., 1979. U.S. Department of Commerce, Bureau of the Census, Statistical Abstract of the United States, 1978.

market activities at home. Thus, to establish the imputed value of housework over time, five times the number of working hours of persons employed in self-service stores, laundries, etc. has been deducted from the total number of hours required for housework activities each year. However, if the Robinson hypothesis were to be accepted, namely that there was a drastic cut in hours of family care at least between 1965 and 1975, this would result in accepting also a higher and dynamically rising productivity for such activities when taking place in the market. In that case, the imputed value of housework would be less than the figure already calculated in the EAW-index. Since no such adjustment has been made, any underestimation of the value of free time, which is considered to have remained constant, is offset by a corresponding overestimation of the imputed value of housework. The validity of the preceding line of argument depends on whether the findings of the Robinson survey are representative of overall trends in the U.S. economy.

(e) Public sector services, relating mainly to expenditure on education and health

This is the last item that has to be added to private consumption in order to complete the EAW-index. The approach to this question is similar to that adopted for private expenditure on health and education. The only difference is that the portion of private expenditure which is in the nature of investment or corrective spending is deducted, while in the present case the portion of public expenditure directly contributing to individual well-being is added.

Here also, the problem faced in calculating public expenditure on health and education is that U.S. national accounts make no clear-cut distinction between investment and current spending. For this reason certain assumptions had to be made regarding the portion of total public expenditure which should be reckoned as analogous to a consumer outlay and be included in the EAW-index. In the case of public health expenditure, 50 per cent of the annual increment in per capita real public expenditure on health, supposed to be directly conducive to social welfare, has been added in the EAW-index. The other 50 per cent of the increment has been reckoned as investment or corrective spending. Here again the base year is 1950, in which it is assumed that total public expenditure on health was conducive to social well-being. As regards public education expenditure, half of the current annual public expenditure on college and university education has been considered to be consumer spending with a direct favourable impact on social welfare. The portion of public health and education outlays assumed to contribute directly to social welfare is presented in Table 19.

TABLE 19

Public Consumption

(portion of health and education outlays contributing
to an increase in welfare)

(At 1972 prices)

Year	$ billion	Year	$ billion	Year	$ billion
1950	8.6	1960	12.2	1970	21.2
1951	8.9	1961	12.9	1971	22.5
1952	9.2	1962	13.6	1972	23.2
1953	9.5	1963	14.3	1973	24.0
1954	9.8	1964	15.0	1974	24.4
1955	10.2	1965	15.9	1975	25.4
1956	10.5	1966	16.9	1976	26.5
1957	10.8	1967	17.8	1977	27.0
1958	11.3	1968	18.9		
1959	11.7	1969	20.1		

Data processed from the following source: U.S. Department of Commerce, Bureau of the Census, Statistical Abstract 1978, pp. 99, 135 and 490.

U.S. $ Billion
(At 1972 Prices)

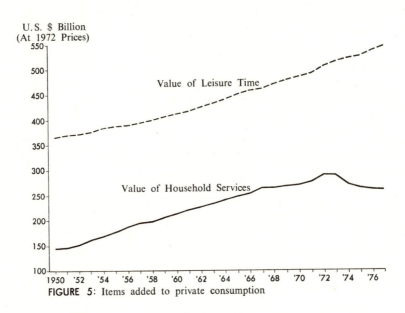

FIGURE 5: Items added to private consumption

U.S. $ Billion
(At 1972 Prices)

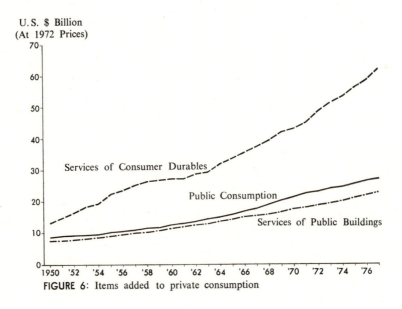

FIGURE 6: Items added to private consumption

Lastly, some direct public welfare expenditures have been entirely dismissed from the EAW-index because, if they are in cash, they are already included in private consumption. If they are in kind, they are probably included for the most part in health expenditure and are therefore taken account of through the method of calculation described in the previous paragraph.

III. SUMMARY OF EMPIRICAL FINDINGS

The foregoing calculations have resulted in the compilation of an EAW-index, whose relationship to GNP is depicted in the cumulative Tables 20-24 and in Figure 7.

This index, which applies to the United States for the period from 1950 to 1977, confirms the primary hypothesis made in this essay, namely that the economic aspects of social welfare are a diminishing function of economic growth in industrially mature, affluent societies. Thus the EAW-index rises at a lower rate than GNP (at 1972 prices). Specifically, while the average annual growth rate of GNP over the study period was 3.4 per cent, the corresponding rate for the EAW-index was 2.2 per cent. This is because the items deducted from private consumption, namely those regarded as having a decremental effect on welfare, grew faster than GNP during the same period. Furthermore, while the value of deductible items represented 15.7 per cent (at constant prices) of GNP in 1950, the ratio rose to 26.8 per cent in 1977. This means that a continually increasing real production cost is required over time for the attainment of a given level of effective consumption. On the other hand, the items which have been added to private consumption dropped in value from 101.4 per cent of GNP in 1950 to 69.0 per cent in 1977. The outcome of these developments was

a steady drop in the ratio of social economic welfare to
GNP at 1972 prices, from 1.49 in 1950 to 1.07 in 1977.
This implies that the increase in economic welfare is smaller
than the corresponding increase in GNP. The above ratio,
however, gives no idea of the speed at which each of the
magnitudes involved changes over time. To depict more
precisely the forces affecting the respective rates of change
use has been made of the concept of elasticity, i.e. of the
percentage change in economic welfare in response to a given
percentage change in GNP. Examination of the "national
product elasticity of economic welfare" suggests a systematic
decline in the rate of increase in economic welfare in relation to the rate of economic growth over the study period.
Specifically, the percentage increase in the EAW-index, in
response to given percentage increases in GNP, fell from
0.717 during the period 1950–1960 to 0.639 during the
period 1960–1970 and 0.547 during the period 1970–1977.
These elasticities were obtained without deduction of the
imputed cost of use of natural resources. When this element
was considered in the compilation of the EAW-index, the
results remained virtually unaltered, i.e., the trend value of
the elasticity of economic welfare with respect to changes in
national product kept falling. The corresponding elasticities,
when natural resources were accounted for, became 0.677
in the period 1950–1960, 0.583 in the period 1960–1970
and 0.511 in the period 1970–1977 (Table 22).

   These numerical values underline the original argument,
namely that percentage increases in social welfare over time
are smaller than the corresponding increases in GNP and
are diminishing. It may be calculated that, *ceteris paribus*,
within a mere twenty-five to thirty years from now the elasticity measure will reach or come very close to zero. The
implication is that, when the EAW/GNP elasticity reaches
zero, economic welfare will have attained its maximum

value. Beyond that point of bliss, any further increase in GNP would lead to an absolute decline in economic welfare, since the projection of relevant magnitudes on the basis of past trends gives a negative elasticity of economic welfare from around the first decade of the next century.

The foregoing inference is valid, although the present level of economic welfare is clearly overestimated. This is so, because it is obvious that damage costs, for instance, are much higher than they are made to appear by the inadequacy of available data. It is also obvious that the socio-economic and political repercussions of a virtually permanent energy crisis cannot be depicted solely in market prices, despite their considerable rise after 1973.

Hence the relationship established in this essay between the economic aspects of welfare and economic growth, as well as the increasing divergence between these two variables over time, understate the real dimensions of the problem and lessen its acuteness.[67]

TABLE 20

Magnitudes Forming the EAW-Index

($ billion, at 1972 prices)

Year	Gross National Product at market prices	Private consumption	Private expenditure on consumer durables	Private expenditure on advertising	Cost of resource depletion	Cost of environmental pollution (private)	Private cost of commuting
1950	533.5	338.1	43.4	6.0	—	23.0	8.8
1951	576.5	342.3	39.9	6.5	0.8	25.2	10.0
1952	598.5	350.9	38.9	6.8	0.2	26.3	11.1
1953	621.8	364.2	43.1	7.0	0.8	27.6	12.5
1954	613.7	370.9	43.5	7.2	2.2	27.8	13.4
1955	654.8	395.1	52.2	7.8	2.5	30.5	15.6
1956	668.8	406.3	49.8	8.3	3.2	32.0	17.9
1957	680.9	414.7	49.7	8.3	5.8	33.4	19.8
1958	679.5	419.0	46.4	8.0	7.1	33.5	21.3
1959	720.4	441.5	51.8	8.6	10.2	36.2	23.8
1960	736.8	453.0	52.5	8.8	12.1	37.5	26.3
1961	755.3	462.2	50.3	8.6	13.4	39.4	28.3
1962	799.1	482.9	55.7	8.8	15.9	42.6	31.1
1963	830.7	501.4	60.7	9.2	18.1	45.1	33.7
1964	874.4	528.7	65.7	9.8	20.9	48.7	37.0
1965	925.9	558.1	73.4	10.3	24.0	52.7	40.7
1966	981.0	586.1	79.0	10.9	28.1	57.2	44.3
1967	1,007.7	603.2	79.7	10.7	30.3	60.2	48.2
1968	1,051.8	633.4	88.2	11.1	33.9	64.2	52.4
1969	1,078.8	655.4	91.9	11.3	37.5	67.8	57.1
1970	1,075.3	668.9	88.9	10.8	40.3	58.2	60.7
1971	1,107.5	691.9	98.1	10.8	43.8	58.8	64.9
1972	1,171.1	733.0	111.2	11.7	50.0	63.2	71.6
1973	1,235.0	767.7	121.8	12.0	58.5	66.7	77.7
1974	1,217.8	760.7	112.5	11.8	39.7	63.8	80.2
1975	1,202.3	774.6	112.7	11.5	40.2	65.8	81.0
1976	1,271.0	819.4	125.9	12.8	49.3	68.6	87.9
1977	1,332.7	857.7	137.8	13.5	55.7	71.0	95.4

TABLE 20 *(continued)*

Magnitudes Forming the EAW-Index

(\$ billion, at 1972 prices)

Private expenditure on health (not raising the level of welfare)	Private expenditure on education (not raising the level of welfare)	Services from public buildings included in the EAW-index	Imputed value of services from consumer durables	Imputed value of household services	Imputed value of leisure time	Public health and education outlays contributing to welfare
—	2.7	7.5	13.2	143.4	368.4	8.6
—	2.7	7.8	14.9	146.5	371.5	8.9
0.1	2.7	8.1	16.4	153.5	376.1	9.2
0.3	2.8	8.4	18.2	163.9	378.5	9.5
0.8	3.0	8.8	19.7	170.1	385.9	9.8
1.1	3.3	9.1	22.5	179.9	387.0	10.2
1.5	3.4	9.5	23.9	189.8	390.1	10.5
2.0	3.5	10.0	25.2	195.9	396.2	10.8
2.3	3.9	10.5	26.2	199.7	402.9	11.3
2.9	4.0	11.0	26.8	208.5	408.3	11.7
4.4	4.8	11.5	27.1	215.2	412.9	12.2
4.9	5.1	12.0	27.5	220.8	419.3	12.9
6.2	5.5	12.6	28.7	229.2	425.2	13.6
6.9	5.8	13.0	29.6	234.3	433.7	14.3
8.8	5.9	13.8	32.0	241.7	442.4	15.0
9.6	6.5	14.5	33.9	249.3	451.2	15.9
10.5	7.1	15.1	35.8	253.9	458.0	16.9
11.0	7.5	15.6	37.4	266.4	463.6	17.8
12.3	8.3	16.2	39.7	266.1	472.1	18.9
14.3	8.8	16.8	42.0	269.8	480.0	20.1
16.0	9.2	17.5	43.0	270.1	485.6	21.2
17.3	9.7	18.2	45.2	278.0	493.9	22.5
20.1	10.1	18.9	48.3	290.9	507.2	23.2
22.8	10.3	19.7	51.7	290.0	517.9	24.0
24.1	10.0	20.5	53.2	271.9	524.6	24.4
25.6	10.1	21.3	56.2	264.4	526.9	25.4
28.0	10.5	22.1	58.6	261.6	538.0	26.5
29.1	10.7	23.0	62.1	260.7	547.2	27.0

TABLE 21

The EAW-Index and its Ratio to GNP

($ billion, at 1972 prices)

Year	Gross National Product at market prices	Private consumption	Total of deductible items (without resource depletion cost)	Total of deductible items (with resource depletion cost)	Total of additive items
1950	533.5	338.1	83.9	83.9	541.1
1951	576.5	342.3	84.3	85.1	549.6
1952	598.5	350.9	85.9	86.1	563.3
1953	621.8	364.2	93.3	94.1	578.5
1954	613.7	370.9	95.7	97.9	594.3
1955	654.8	395.1	110.5	113.0	608.7
1956	668.8	406.3	112.9	116.1	623.8
1957	680.9	414.7	116.7	122.5	638.1
1958	679.5	419.0	115.4	122.5	650.6
1959	720.4	441.5	127.3	137.5	666.3
1960	736.8	453.0	134.3	146.4	678.9
1961	755.3	462.2	136.6	150.0	692.5
1962	799.1	482.9	149.9	165.8	709.3
1963	830.7	501.4	161.4	179.5	724.9
1964	874.4	528.7	175.9	196.8	744.9
1965	925.9	558.1	193.2	217.2	764.8
1966	981.0	586.1	209.0	237.1	779.7
1967	1,007.7	603.2	217.3	247.6	800.8
1968	1,051.8	633.4	236.5	270.4	813.0
1969	1,078.8	655.4	251.2	288.7	828.7
1970	1,075.3	668.9	243.8	284.1	837.4
1971	1,107.5	691.9	259.6	303.4	857.8
1972	1,171.1	733.0	287.9	337.9	888.5
1973	1,235.0	767.7	311.3	369.8	903.3
1974	1,217.8	760.7	302.4	342.1	894.6
1975	1,202.3	774.6	306.7	346.9	894.2
1976	1,271.0	819.4	333.7	383.0	906.8
1977	1,332.7	857.7	357.5	413.2	920.0

EAW-Index$_1$: Excluding cost of resource depletion.

EAW-Index$_2$: Including cost of resource depletion.

TABLE 21 *(continued)*

The EAW-Index and its Ratio to GNP

($ billion, at 1972 prices)

EAW- Index$_1$	EAW- Index$_2$	Ratio of EAW- Index$_1$ to GNP	Ratio of EAW- Index$_2$ to GNP
795.3	795.3	1.491	1.491
807.6	806.8	1.401	1.399
828.3	828.1	1.384	1.384
849.4	848.6	1.366	1.365
869.5	867.3	1.417	1.413
893.3	890.8	1.364	1.360
917.2	914.0	1.371	1.367
936.1	930.3	1.375	1.366
954.2	947.1	1.404	1.394
980.5	970.3	1.361	1.347
997.6	985.5	1.354	1.338
1,018.1	1,004.7	1.348	1.330
1,042.3	1,026.4	1.304	1.284
1,064.9	1,046.8	1.282	1.260
1,097.7	1,076.8	1.255	1.231
1,129.7	1,105.7	1.220	1.194
1,156.8	1,128.7	1.179	1.151
1,186.7	1,156.4	1.178	1.148
1,209.9	1,176.0	1.150	1.118
1,232.9	1,195.4	1.143	1.108
1,262.5	1,222.2	1.174	1.137
1,290.1	1,246.3	1.165	1.125
1,333.6	1,283.6	1.139	1.096
1,359.7	1,301.2	1.101	1.054
1,352.9	1,313.2	1.111	1.078
1,362.1	1,321.9	1.133	1.099
1,392.5	1,343.2	1.096	1.057
1,420.2	1,364.5	1.066	1.024

TABLE 22

Economic Welfare Elasticity with Respect to GNP

	1950–1960	1960–1970	1970–1977
— Percentage change in EAW-index$_1$ / percentage change in GNP	0.717	0.639	0.547
— Percentage change in EAW-index$_2$ / percentage change in GNP	0.677	0.583	0.511

EAW - Index$_1$: Excluding cost of resource depletion.
EAW - Index$_2$: Including cost of resource depletion.
The above elasticities were obtained by using the annual mean values of GNP and EAW-index.

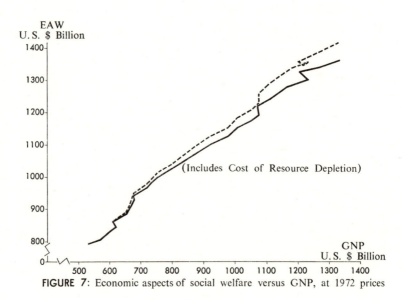

FIGURE 7: Economic aspects of social welfare versus GNP, at 1972 prices

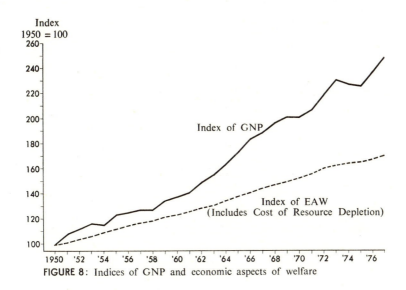

FIGURE 8: Indices of GNP and economic aspects of welfare

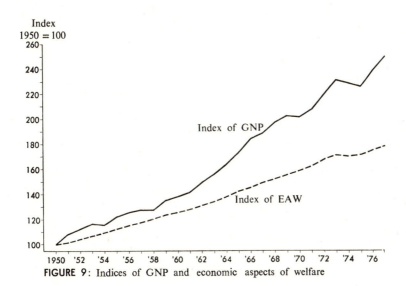

FIGURE 9: Indices of GNP and economic aspects of welfare

TABLE 23

GNP and Items Included in the EAW-Index

(Average annual growth rates)

	1950-1960	1960-1970	1970-1977
—GNP at market prices	3.3	3.9	3.1
—Private consumption	3.0	4.0	3.6
—Deductible items (A)	4.8	6.1	5.6
—Deductible items (B)	5.7	6.9	5.5
—Private consumption minus deductible items (A)	2.3	2.9	2.3
—Private consumption minus deductible items (B)	1.9	2.3	2.1
—Additive items	2.3	2.1	1.4
—EAW-index$_1$ (Private consumption minus deductible items (A) plus additive items)	2.3	2.4	1.7
—EAW-index$_2$ (Private consumption minus deductible items (B) plus additive items)	2.2	2.2	1.6

(A) Without resource depletion cost.
(B) With resource depletion cost.

TABLE 24

Items to Be Deducted from or Added to Private Consumption, as a Percentage of GNP

(At 1972 prices)

	1950	1955	1960	1965	1970	1975	1977
DEDUCTIBLE ITEMS: (without resource depletion cost)	15.7	16.9	18.3	20.8	22.7	25.5	26.8
a. Private expenditure on consumer durables	8.1	8.0	7.1	7.9	8.3	9.4	10.3
b. Private expenditure on advertising	1.1	1.2	1.2	1.1	1.0	1.0	1.0
c. Cost of resource depletion	—	0.4	1.6	2.6	3.7	3.3	4.2
d. Cost of environmental pollution (private)	4.3	4.6	5.1	5.7	5.4	5.5	5.3
e. Cost of commuting	1.7	2.4	3.6	4.4	5.6	6.7	7.2
f. Private expenditure on health (waste)	—	0.2	0.6	1.0	1.5	2.1	2.2
g. Private expenditure on education, not raising the level of welfare	0.5	0.5	0.7	0.7	0.9	0.8	0.8
DEDUCTIBLE ITEMS: (with resource depletion cost)	15.7	17.3	19.9	23.4	26.4	28.8	31.0
ADDITIVE ITEMS:	101.4	93.0	92.1	82.6	77.9	74.4	69.0
a. Flow of services from public buildings, included in the EAW-index	1.4	1.4	1.5	1.6	1.6	1.8	1.7
b. Services from consumer durables	2.5	3.4	3.7	3.7	4.0	4.7	4.7
c. Value of household services	26.9	27.5	29.2	26.9	25.1	22.0	19.6
d. Value of leisure time	69.0	59.1	56.0	48.7	45.2	43.8	41.0
e. Public health and education outlays contributing to welfare	1.6	1.6	1.7	1.7	2.0	2.1	2.0

NOTES

TO CHAPTER THREE

1. During the last few years, the compilation of an index that would measure economic welfare better than national accounting data do has been the subject of numerous studies, at both the academic and the empirical level. Thus, G. Myrdal in *Against the Stream — Critical Essays on Economics,* (New York, Vintage Books, 1975) discusses the weaknesses of GNP to be used as a realistic index of social welfare. He realises though that attempts to correct the GNP figures would cause serious problems of arbitrariness etc.; E. Malinvaud, in "Costs of Economic Growth" (*Economic Growth and Resources,* ed. E. Malinvaud, London, Macmillan, 1979), realises also the difficulties involved in any attempt to construct a "corrected GNP" (p. 189). He argues, however, in favour of the incorporation of "misgivings about the cost of economic growth into the theory of optimum growth" (*ibid.,* p. 204).

At the empirical level, one of the first economists to have diagnosed the inefficiency of national income accounts as proxies for the measurement of economic welfare is A. W. Sametz ("Production of Goods and Services: The Measurement of Economic Growth," *Indicators of Social Change,* eds. E. Sheldon and W. Moore, New York, Russell Sage Foundation, 1968). According to him, a more exact evaluation would require the inclusion of social " 'nonpriced' costs, such as pollution, and of the previously nonpriced (i.e., nonmarketed) output of a 'domestic' or handicraft system" (p. 79).

Furthermore, Sametz proceeded to the calculation of the United States' Net National Product of the period 1869-1966, corrected for increases in leisure time. For the development of a "welfare output" indicator, he suggested a reworking of the existing time series to include items such as leisure time or a "quality improvement" factor, and exclude major social cost items. What is more important, however, is that he recognised that the construction of a "net output index" is nothing more than a specification "of the measurable part of economic welfare." For the formation of a more complete index of social welfare and happiness, he proposed the inclusion of an "Index of Absolutes" (such as average per capita life expectancy, years of schooling, etc.), and an "Index of Consumer Wealth" including stocks of housing, cars, financial assets, etc.

In the early 1970s, K. Boulding pointed to the possibility of concurrence of adverse side-effects in the process of further economic growth, which would ultimately diminish social welfare.

In "What Do Economic Indicators Indicate?: Quality and Quantity in the GNP" (*Economics of Pollution,* New York, New York University Press, 1971), Boulding argued that "an increase in a [GNP] does not, in fact, increase V [Social Welfare Function], perhaps on the Aristotelian Mean principle that beyond a certain point it is bad for people to get richer. A rise in a creates, shall we say, a rise in b, which is pollution, which operates to diminish V, or a rise in c, which is vulgarity, which also operates to diminish V, or a fall in d, which is equality, which also operates to diminish V, and so on. The sum of all these movements may diminish V, whereas we might still think that a simple rise in the GNP would raise it" (p. 52).

What Boulding suggests is the need to improve National Income Statistics by taking account of items like household production, and by including "bads" and separating public from private goods (*ibid.*, p. 79).

F. Juster in "A Framework for the Measurement of Economic and Social Performance" (*The Measurement of Economic and Social Performance,* ed. Milton Moss, New York, National Bureau of Economic Research, 1973), discusses the inadequacies of the national income and product accounts, and proposes a framework for economic and social accounts. Such a framework should include both tangible and intangible reproducible wealth, together with human, natural physical resources, and sociopolitical wealth.

In the same collection of essays, there is the pioneering paper of W. Nordhaus and J. Tobin "Is Growth Obsolete?", which in many respects has served as a guideline for the compilation of the Index of the Economic Aspects of Welfare of the present study.

Here again, the fundamental observation is made, namely that both the GNP and the NNP cannot be used as satisfactory measures of welfare, since they are meant to measure production. Tobin and Nordhaus proceed to the construction of a Measure of Economic Welfare (MEW). From this measure, regrettable or instrumental expenditures are excluded, on the reasoning that they "... are among the necessary overhead costs of a complex industrial nation-state..." while it is recognised that it is practically impossible to draw the line between final and instrumental outlays *(ibid.,* pp. 515-16).

As far as health and education outlays are concerned, they are treated as investment. That is, they are regarded as indirect rather than direct sources of consumer satisfaction and they are thus omitted from the Measure of Economic Welfare. On the other hand, the value of leisure time and of nonmarket activities is positively included in the MEW, while alternative assumptions are made regarding productivity changes in these items. Finally, the disamenities of urbanisation are calculated on the basis of a cross-section analysis concerning the higher income ("premium") that is necessary to hold people in densely populated areas.

It has to be noted that no calculations are made for the social cost of pollution and environmental deterioration; as far as resource exhaustion is concerned, Tobin and Nordhaus assumed continuous substitutability between natural resources and other factors of production.

The basic result of the Tobin-Nordhaus method is that "...per capita MEW has been growing more slowly than per capita NNP (1.1 per cent for MEW as against 1.7 per cent for NNP, at annual rates over the period 1929-1965). Yet MEW has been growing. The progress indicated by conventional national accounts is not just a myth that evaporates when a welfare-oriented measure is substituted" (*ibid.,* p. 521).

A similar study, for the calculation of a Net National Welfare (NNW) index for Japan and for the years 1955, 1960, 1965 and 1970, was made by the Japanese NNW Measurement Committee, under the general directorship of Miyohei Shinohara. A major difference between the latter study and the paper by Tobin and Nordhaus is that the NNW Measurement Committee makes allowance for the cost of pollution, an item that appears under two headings, first as "environmental maintenance cost", which comprises internalised expenditures to protect the natural environment from pollution, and second as "environmental pollution cost", which consists of the huge external damage cost of pollution.

The result of the work of the NNW Measurement Committee is that, at 1970 prices, the ratio of Net National Welfare (NNW) over Net Domestic Product (NDP) (excluding net investment) falls throughout the 1950-1970 period, both when leisure time and nonmarket activities are included in NNW and when they are excluded from it.

In a paper by S. F. Singer and B. W. Perry ("The Economic Effects of Demographic Changes"), which deals primarily with the way alternative fertility scenarios affect economic growth, an index of welfare, the Q-index, is defined as a measure of per capita consumption, less instrumental expenditures (p. 15). For the compilation of the Q-index, all the goods and services which contribute directly to economic and "societal" welfare — like food, clothing, shelter, recreation and personal services — are added together. Conversely, items like investment expenditures, expenditures for pollution control and resource development, together with "instrumental expenditures" (regrettable necessities) such as defence, police, commuting to work, etc., are excluded. Moreover, the Q-index comprises items such as nonmarket activities and leisure time, though in a corrective (and not extensive) sense.

In his study "Measures of Leisure, Equality and Welfare" (OECD, Paris 1978), Wilfred Beckerman discusses the question of whether conventional GNP reflects the true growth of economic welfare. For this purpose, Beckerman tries an alternative indicator, the Measurable Economic Welfare (MEW), which takes account of leisure and income distribution. Beckerman's decision to include the value of leisure in MEW was motivated by the above-mentioned Tobin-Nordhaus study, where leisure seems to have had "a far greater impact on their estimates [i.e., of Tobin and Nordhaus] than any other of the items that they included..." (p. 3).

Estimates of MEW including leisure were made for thirteen advanced countries and for the period 1950-1952 to 1971-1973. The results obtained depend largely on whether leisure is assumed to be subject to productivity increases or not. Thus "...if no productivity increase is attributed to leisure, the growth of MEW will inevitably be much slower than that of GNP... whereas if leisure is credited with a rise in productivity equal to the rise in the real wage, the growth of MEW will not differ much from that of GNP" (*ibid.,* p. 14). In either case, however "...there is a fairly close correlation between the ranking of countries according to GNP growth rates and their ranking according to MEW..." (p. 23). With regard to income distribution, Beckerman uses the concept of "equally distributed income" (p. 42). This method is applied for nine countries and the outcome is that, over the period in question, "...there has been no significant change in income distribution whatever measure one uses to evaluate the change" (p. 47).

The overall result of the MEW approach is that "...GNP is a fairly good indicator of relative growth of measurable economic welfare and that when other quantifiable items are added they do not have any very significant effect on relative performance over the period covered..." (p. 52).

2. In his article "The Valuation of the Social Income" (*Economica,* Vol. VII, [May 1940]), Professor J. R. Hicks stressed the need to differentiate social product as a measure of economic welfare from social product as a measure of productivity.

3. "The National Income and Product Accounts of the United States are thus basically designed to provide an efficient measure of cyclical changes in total activity. In such a framework, the focus is on flows of inputs and outputs; stocks of assets are important only insofar as they cause cyclical movements in the related flows" (Juster, *op. cit.,* p. 30).

"The accounts do, of course, serve the purpose for which they were designed: to measure the current state of the nation, uncover the proximate causes of economic fluctuations, and suggest countercyclical policies... But change in GNP over long periods of time is not a good measure of economic growth or welfare" (Sametz, *op. cit.*, p. 77).

4. The term "intermediate" denotes goods and services which are simply a means to satisfaction of wants for final goods. (Fred Hirsch, *Social Limits to Growth*, Cambridge, Mass., Harvard University Press, 1976, p. 56.)

It may be said that defensive goods and services, or regrettable necessities, are a version of intermediate goods in the sense that they derive their importance from the negative factors that must be countered. "If the risk of fire rises, additional fire stations will make economic output higher than it would be without them, but production, in the sense of net or final product, will be no higher than in the period when the danger of fire was less" (*ibid.*, p. 57).

5. Certain goods in this category are strongly in the nature of investment. Thus, when a consumer chooses, for instance, to purchase a specific model of car, his choice is influenced not only by price and personal taste, but also by the resale value of the car. The same goes for other consumer durables, particularly those subject to technological obsolescence, such as electronic equipment. In such cases, these goods are bought not only for consumption but also as an investment. Even in the former case, the welfare of the consumer does not increase momentarily, but extends over a considerably lengthier period. "The most important of these [durables], cars and houses, are bought not only for consumption but also as an investment for their resale value; and buying for high resale value means buying not what one wants but what one believes other people want." (Tibor Scitovsky, *Papers on Welfare and Growth*, London, Allen & Unwin, 1964, p. 247.)

6. It cannot be denied that we run out of resources in a physical sense. The question is if we run out of resources in an economic sense. Harold Barnett and Chandler Morse *(Scarcity and Growth —The Economics of Natural Resource Availability*, Baltimore, Johns Hopkins University Press, 1969) do not accept the pessimistic view. Examining the hypothesis that economic scarcity of natural resources as measured by the trend of real cost of extractive output will increase over time, they have found that for the United States and for the period 1870-1957 the unit cost of extractive products was declining. This reduction of unit costs was due to technological progress and to the fact that, with few exceptions, new reserves of minerals have been discovered. The scarcity hypothesis is contradicted, among others, by the studies of O. C. Herfindahl *(Copper Costs and Prices: 1870-1957,* Baltimore, Johns Hopkins University

Press, 1959, and *Three Studies in Mineral Economics,* Washington: Resources for the Future, 1961), who finds no upward trends in real costs for copper and other minerals, and of W. Nordhaus ("Resources as a Constraint on Growth," *American Economic Review,* Vol. LXIV, [May 1974], p. 24), who finds that the prices of eleven minerals have fallen relative to the price of labour since 1900.

However, according to Frederick M. Peterson and Anthony C. Fisher ("The Exploitation of Extractive Resources – A Survey," *Economic Journal,* [December 1977], p. 706), there is no guarantee that the behaviour of costs and prices will be the same over the next hundred years as it has been in the past. Moreover, V. Kerry Smith in his "Measuring Natural Resource Scarcity: Theory and Practice" *(Journal of Environmental Economics and Management,* 5, 1978) seriously questions the validity of the Barnett-Morse pioneering study, at least for the post-1957 (to 1973) period. The "misbehaviour" of Barnett-Morse tests when applied to recent data led Smith to conclude that the scarcity problem remains an open issue.

Even if it is accepted that the costs of natural resources are declining over time, the scarcity hypothesis is not removed from the economic scene. Since lower costs and prices lead to higher consumption, the depletion of the reserves must have been faster.

Here it must be stressed that scarcity — even in the economic and not the physical sense — has to be thought of in connection with the required standard of the resource to be used, especially from the environmental quality point of view. Characteristic in this respect is the case of coal. In the United States, for instance, coal reserves are so abundant that that country was called, after the Arab oil embargo, the "Persian Gulf of Coal". Yet, although coal constitutes about 90 per cent of total U.S. energy resources and its reserves are expected to last for at least another century, this mineral provided in the late 1970s only 18 per cent of total U.S. energy production. It seems that, although "the United States has an abundance of coal, coal in turn has an abundance of problems," the most important being of course the problem of environmental pollution. "Coal possesses the troublesome attribute of generating a seemingly endless string of environmental hazards that are ubiquitous and pervasive. As soon as one hazard, such as sulfur dioxide emissions, is identified and solved, it seems that another possible environmental danger associated with coal, such as carbon dioxide emissions, becomes a source of controversy." Problems exist "at practically every part of the coal system," from the moment of underground mining to the moment of consumption, when emissions of sulfur dioxide, nitrogen oxide, trace elements and carbon dioxide are poured into the atmosphere. Moreover, waterways are contaminated by thermal and chemical discharges, while coal ash creates problems of solid-waste disposal. The most serious hazard, however, of burning coal seems to be the "greenhouse effect", caused by the emission of carbon dioxide into the atmosphere. In 1977, the U.S. National Academy of Sciences warned that "the climatic effects of carbon dioxide release may be the primary limiting factor on energy production from fossil fuels over the next few centuries." Environmental problems caused by massive use of coal could be minimised if new, cleaner technologies were used — such as the fluidized-bed combustion or the gasification and liquefaction of coal. Liquefaction in particular seems to be the most promising among the new coal technologies. It seems, however, that "liquefied or gasified coal is much more expensive than petroleum or natural gas." Thus, although increasing amounts are spent on research and development in this field, existing problems preclude coal from becoming the transitional energy resource, no matter how plentiful its reserves may be. (*Energy Future,* Report of the Energy Project at the Harvard Business School, eds. Robert Stobaugh and Daniel Yergin, New York, Random House, 1979, pp. 79-104, *passim.*)

7. The need for an effective differentiation in the prices of non-renewable resources to take account of the time factor has long been recognised. Alfred Marshall's views on this subject are typical in the sense that he stressed the distinction that must be made between "farmer's rent" and "mining rent" (A. Marshall, *Principles of Economics*, 8th ed., London, Macmillan, 1952, p. 139).

"...The produce of the field is something other than the soil; for the field, properly cultivated, retains its fertility. But the produce of the mine is part of the mine itself... This difference is illustrated by the fact that the rent of a mine is calculated on a different principle from that of a farm... and, while the farmer's rent is reckoned by the year, mining rent consists chiefly of 'royalties' which are levied in proportion to the stores that are taken out of nature's storehouse."

It seems, however, that he entertained considerable doubts as to whether this can be done with any degree of accuracy. "But the royalty itself on a ton of coal, when accurately adjusted, represents that diminution in the value of the mine, regarded as a source of wealth in the future, which is caused by taking the ton out of nature's storehouse" (*ibid.*, p. 364).

The basis of the current analysis of optimal management of an exhaustible resource over time is the work of H. Hotelling "The Economics of Exhaustible Resources" (*Journal of Political Economy*, Vol. 39, [April 1931], No. 2, p. 137). On this subject, see also Robert Solow, "The Economics of Resources or the Resources of Economics, R. T. Ely Lecture," *American Economic Review,*

Vol. LXIV, (May 1974), pp. 1-14; William Nordhaus, "World Dynamics: Measurement without Data," *Economic Journal*, (December 1973a); Geoffrey Heal, "The Long-run Movement of the Prices of Exhaustible Resources," *Economic Growth and Resources*, ed. E. Malinvaud, Vol. 1, London, Macmillan, 1979, pp. 89-107.

8. W. Nordhaus, "Resources as a Constraint on Growth," *op. cit.*, pp. 22-26.

9. Geoffrey Heal, "The Long-run Movement of the Prices of Exhaustible Resources," *op. cit.*, p. 91.

10. W. Nordhaus, "The Allocation of Energy Resources," Brookings Papers on Economic Activity, 1973a, 3.

11. R. Solow, "Intergenerational Equity and Exhaustible Resources," *Review of Economic Studies*, 1974b.

12. "Over the postwar period, after correcting for changes in the purchasing power of the dollar, the prices of these fuels actually fell; in the case of natural gas, the real price fell *substantially*. All of this has encouraged profligate use of fuel, discouraged exploration for natural gas, and depleted the domestic reserves of inexpensive petroleum... The low prices of energy to producers and consumers in the United States has generated a highly energy-intensive economy" (William J. Baumol and Wallace E. Oates, *Economics, Environmental Policy and the Quality of Life*, Englewood Cliffs, N.J., Prentice-Hall, 1979, p. 116).

13. The inability of the price mechanism to reflect realistically the time dimension of the existing stock of liquid fuels is partly attributed to the operation of a dynamic oligopsony until 1973.

14. It is worth noting that nearly 86 per cent of world energy consumption is confined between the 30th and the 60th parallel in the northern hemisphere, while 71 per cent of the earth's population inhabiting the countries of the so-called Third World consumes only 16 per cent of totally available energy resources *(Reshaping the International Order*, A Report to the Club of Rome, New York, Dutton, 1976, pp. 12 and 38).

North America, with only 6 per cent of the world population, accounts for 30 per cent of the total energy consumed *(Mankind at the Turning Point*, The Second Report to the Club of Rome, London, Hutchinson, 1975, pp. 135-36).

It could therefore be said that, even if the world's oil supply were five times larger than the quantity estimated in the early seventies, it would be entirely depleted within a mere fifty years or so if total energy consumption grew by 3.9 per cent a year, which is rather conservative considering the growth rates of the previous decade *(The Limits to Growth,* A Report to the Club of Rome, New York, Universe Books, 1972, Table 4, pp. 56-59).

15. A. Lovins, "Energy Resources", U.N. Symposium on Population, Resources and Environment, Stockholm 1973, from the article by Ronald G. Ridker in the *American Economic Association,* (May 1974), p. 34.

16. Plutonium-239, which has a radioactive life of more than 24,000 years and which is used primarily in nuclear fission, is an exceedingly dangerous, cancer-inducing substance. Should nuclear (plutonium) reactors constitute the main source of energy in the year 2000, the plutonium content of the atmosphere would be a million times more than needed to exterminate life on our planet. The problem posed by the use of plutonium and other nuclear fission materials with a long life span is basically a moral problem of universal importance outweighing technological expertise (*Le Rapport de Tokyo, sur l'homme et la croissance,* Club de Rome, Paris, Éditions du Seuil, 1974, pp. 31-32).

17. *Reshaping the International Order, op. cit.,* pp. 250-51.

18. The amount of energy received annually by the earth from the sun is 30 times more than known world reserves of coal (1972 data). Thus, in 1970 man-derived energy was less than 0.004 per cent of solar radiation energy. It has been estimated, however, that in order to ensure 4 kW of energy per capita (present French level) for a future population of 10 billion, the land area necessary for obtaining the required solar energy would be 1 per cent of the earth's total surface. This percentage is not difficult to find among regions of a geographical latitude between $+30^0$ and -30^0, i.e. regions with a lot of sunshine. The problem, however, still exists for developed regions in Northern Europe, North America and elsewhere; it is a problem of transporting energy over very long distances. The solution might lie in the development of hydrogen technology; hydrogen may be produced at the solar centres by catalysis or electrolysis and transported from countries of solar energy conversion to the rest of the world *(Stratégie pour demain,* 2e Rapport au Club de Rome, Paris, Éditions du Seuil, 1974, p. 149).

19. The entropy law (the second law of thermodynamics) suggests that the amount of energy bound within a closed system continuously increases; as a result, there is a gradual shift from low entropy (large free energy) to high entropy (large bound energy). The thermodynamic balance of such a system is restored when all free energy is converted into bound energy

(Nicholas Georgescu-Roegen, *The Entropy Law and the Economic Process,* Cambridge, Mass., Harvard University Press, 1976; also, by the same author, "The Entropy Law and the Economic Problem," in *Toward a Steady- State Economy,* ed. Herman Daly, San Francisco, Freeman, 1973, pp. 39-41).

20. Industrial development keeps man off from using energy inflows in favour of the use of the depletable resources of terrestrial energy. Note for instance the industrialisation of agriculture: whereas formerly man used the inflow of the photosynthesis of chlorophyll (i.e. terrestrial flora) as the moving force for oxen, today, in order to move tractors, he is using the depletable resources of terrestrial energy (oil), i.e. energy of high entropy (see N. Georgescu-Roegen).

The above do not, of course, suggest that human history should stop at the age of the plough. However, in the present ecosystem, the faster the rate of economic growth, the faster given forms of terrestrial energy are depleted; the result is thermodynamic balance "where every form of energy will be bound and world order will be converted into ataxia." The introduction of the second law of thermodynamics in economic matters focuses attention on "the price man has to pay for the unique privilege of being able to go beyond the biological limits in his struggle for life" (N. Georgescu-Roegen, "The Entropy Law and the Economic Problem," *op. cit.,* p. 47).

These comments were made long before the recent energy crisis and denote that economic growth, realised without any restrictions or qualitative specifications, may constitute a menace and a curse not only for future generations but for the very generation of the "economic miracle" which was fool enough to base its welfare and activities on oil technology.

21. "The 'cornucopians' argue that most of the essential raw materials are in infinite supply : that as society exhausts one raw material, it will turn to lower-grade, inexhaustible substitutes. Eventually, society will subsist on renewable resources and on elements, such as iron and aluminum, that are practically inexhaustible... This asymptotic society we call the Age of Substitutability." (H. E. Goeller and A. M. Weinberg, "The Age of Substitutability," *American Economic Review,* [December 1978], p. 1.)

Substitution and recycling will be taken care of by the price mechanism and some intervention in the form of appropriately allocating research funds.

The possibilities of re-using scarce resources should not be underestimated. Of course, it is true that, owing to the entropy law, we cannot re-use the whole amount of a resource more than once. Some part of it is dissipated and cannot be regained. However, depending on how carefully we use the resources, we can always multiply them by recycling. Thus, if we assume that λ is the part of a resource which can be re-used after each use, then the total use x of the resource will be:

$$x = w + \lambda Q + \lambda^2 Q + \ldots + \lambda^n Q + \ldots (1)$$

where Q is the amount of resource initially available. Simple manipulation of (1) yields:

$$x = \frac{1-\lambda^n}{1-\lambda} \cdot Q \quad (2)$$

which gives the cumulative use of the resource after n uses. If we let n tend to infinity, we obtain the familiar multiplier formula:

$$x = \frac{1}{1-\lambda} \cdot Q \quad (3).$$

Of course, it is not realistic to believe that we can continue to use parts of a resource *ad infinitum*, as implied by (3). The costs of re-using it in the form of the required energy for that re-use may ultimately become prohibitive, compared with the attained results. We should, therefore, expect to be able to use it a limited number of times, as implied by (2), the truncated multiplier formula. We believe that research and development can equip us with knowledge to increase both λ and n and, consequently, raise the multiplier coefficient.

22. "This difficulty throws doubt upon most of the evaluations worked out so far, for they all rest upon hazardous assumptions. This is no reason, of course, for setting the question aside. On the contrary, it is so important that we must do our best to define the options open to mankind with regard to the use of the earth's exhaustible resources, so that an at least provisional choice can be made." (E. Malinvaud, "Costs of Economic Growth," in *Economic Growth and Resources*, Vol. 1, London, Macmillan, 1979, p. 195.)

23. See Table 2, p. 24, in "Resources as a Constraint on Growth," *American Economic Review, op. cit.* In that table, W. Nordhaus shows the ratio of the prices of the eleven most important minerals to the price of labour. This ratio indicates that there has been a continuous decline in resource prices over the entire century.

24. *Toward a Steady-State Economy, op. cit.*, p. 15.

25. Recent studies show that fish in the Baltic Sea are threatened with extinction owing to oil pollution which has highly diminished the oxygen content of water in certain areas. In 1969, the U.N. Food and Energy Organisation noticed an absolute decline of world fish production for the first time after 1950, while in most categories of fish caught in the Great Lakes of the U.S. between 1900 and 1970 quantity was 100-1000 times lower (*The Limits to*

Growth, op. cit., Figures on p. 77). Ocean pollution is a tremendous problem : it is known that one-fourth of the oxygen we breathe comes from the photo-synthesis of the phytoplankton in oceans, which is particularly sensitive to the various toxic substances of industrial waste. Oceans constitute an equilibrating factor in climatic extremes; yet, even here, pollution tends to disrupt the balance of nature and turn oceans from a source of life into a vast system of drainage pipes on our planet (*Reshaping the International Order, op. cit.,* p. 41). Some also hold oil pollution in the Mediterranean responsible for the great drought which afflicted West Africa some years ago.

26. Ronald Ridker, *Economic Costs of Air Pollution,* New York, Praeger Press, 1969.

27. *Environmental Quality,* The 10th Annual Report of the CEQ, December 1979, p. 667.

28. Ben-Chieh Liu and Eden Yu, "Physical and Economic Damage Functions for Air Pollutants by Receptor," U.S. Environmental Protection Agency (EPA), September 1976.

29. Baumol and Oates, *op. cit.,* note to Table 2-1, p. 25.

30. CEQ, *Environmental Quality,* 1976, p. 167.

31. A. Kneese, R. Ayres, and R. d'Arge, *Economics and the Environment: A Materials Balance Approach,* Baltimore, Johns Hopkins University Press for RFF, 1970.

32. U.S. Department of Commerce, Bureau of the Census, Statistical Abstract of the United States, 1977, p. 644.

33. Economic Report of the President, U.S. Government Printing Office, Washington, D.C., 1979, p. 216.

34. U.S. Department of Commerce, Bureau of the Census, Statistical Abstract of the United States, 1977, p. 644.

35. The amount of 60 cents a day, which has been considered unchanged in real terms throughout the twenty-eight-year period, rather underestimates the actual figure, since fares must surely have risen in line with the increase in the distance between home and workplace that occurred during the same period.

36. Estimate based on data from the U.S. Statistical Abstracts for the years 1973 and 1974.

37. *Social Indicators 1976,* p. 517. Also, according to the Annals of the American Academy of Political and Social Science, Vol. 453, (January 1981),

p. 76, "At current travel activity levels, we spend about one hour per day per capita traveling... travel time would increase by almost 50 percent by the year 2000."

38. The social cost of commuting must be much higher than the figures presented in Table 12. A major reason for this is the fact that "from 1966 to 1977, 628,000 persons lost their lives on the nation's streets and highways because of motor vehicle accidents — about 1,000 persons per week, an average of one death every 10 minutes." (*Social Indicators III*, U.S. Department of Commerce, Bureau of the Census, [December 1980], p. 159.)

39. So it is throughout the rich, industrialised western world. In all the industrialised democracies, a baby's life expectancy is now about 72-76 years, whether its parents pay 5 per cent of national income (Japan) or nearly twice as much (United States, Sweden) for the privilege.

In almost all, health spending is eating further and further into the national income, without a corresponding rise in general health, or even in human happiness about the quality of medical services ("Your Money or your Life," *The Economist*, November 22, 1980, p. 12).

40. In twelve countries the frequency of occurrence of certain diseases is less than in the United States. A further indication that health conditions in the United States are not commensurable to expenditures is provided by the U.S. infant mortality rate, which dropped from 5th place on the world scale in 1950 to 8th place in 1955, 12th place in 1960 and 14th place in 1964. U.S. Department of Health, Education, and Welfare, *Toward a Social Report*, Introd. by W. J. Cohen, Ann Arbor, University of Michigan Press, 1970, p. 7.

41. *Ibid.*, pp. 6 - 9.

42. At this point it would be interesting to mention certain views on whether the "goods" of health and education are intermediate or final, in other words whether respective expenditures constitute investment or consumption.

The former view is upheld by K. Boulding, F. Juster, J. Tobin, W. Nordhaus, and others. K. Boulding in "What Do Economic Indicators Indicate?" (*op. cit.*, p. 60) criticises Gross National Product because, among other things, "it overestimates economic welfare insofar as it does not take adequate account... of items of personal expenditure which should really be regarded as 'costs' rather than 'income', such as commuting, health maintenance, educational investment, and so on."

In "A Framework for the Measurement of Economic and Social Performance" (*op. cit.*, pp. 73-74), F. Juster argues that the above distinction may hold true of an extensive scale of goods and services. "The problem is best illustrated by asking how to measure final consumption by households... By the most rigid definition, only the surplus of satisfaction-yielding output over all requirements for maintenance of both tangible and human capital stock would be so classified... How far one wants to push this argument is another question... it does seem to me that people go to hospitals because they are sick, not because the food is good and the room is airy and bright... So far as I am concerned, these are pure and simple costs of maintaining a flow of services from assets, and they represent final output only to the degree that they increase the flow of services from those capital assets via net investment."

In particular, as regards the stock of human capital, Juster seems to adopt J. Kendrick's view (as expressed in "The Treatment of Intangible Resources as Capital," *Review of Income and Wealth,* [March 1972]) of investment in intangibles. This category of investment includes "direct schooling costs, foregone earnings of students, business and government outlays for research and development, and investments in health and mobility." *(Ibid.,* pp. 51 and 54.)

Tobin and Nordhaus hold a similar view on expenses for health and education purposes, which they consider as investment expenses, not taking them into consideration when compiling MEW (Measure of Economic Welfare). They, however, accept that there is a partiality error comparable to the consumption component of relevant expenditure. "In the case of educational and health capital, we have assumed the yields to be intermediate services rather than direct consumption; that is, we expect to see the fruits of investments in education and health realized in labor productivity and earnings, and we do not count them twice. Our measure understates economic welfare and its growth to the extent that education and medical care are direct rather than indirect sources of consumer satisfaction." ("Is Growth Obsolete?", *op. cit.,* p. 517.)

The above views were mentioned as illustrative of the human capital approach to education and health. They are, however, strongly contested on grounds similar to the criticism raised by R. Solow: "I don't doubt at all that there is an investment-like element in education, with the return coming in subsequent higher productivity and wages. But I have deliberately said 'investment-like' because it is not precisely clear to me that what education creates is properly a stock... I have the impression that the human capital theorists have tended to ignore — and therefore to underestimate — the consumption component of education." ("A Framework for the Measurement of Economic and Social Performance," *op. cit.,* p. 103.)

S. F. Singer and B. W. Perry ("The Economic Effects of Demographic Changes," *op. cit.*) adopt an intermediate solution, according to which a part of the expenditure on health and education is investment expenses and the other part consumption expenses.

The afore-mentioned study states that an effort is made to assess not total welfare but only "...the quantity of one of the inputs to welfare: consumption" (p. 19). Singer and Perry consider expenses on health to be totally consumption expenditure; they, therefore, include them in their Q-index which is "...a per capita index of 'real' income, a corrected per capita GNP" (p. 21). As regards expenses on education, they consider all expenses on primary and secondary education and 50 per cent of those on higher education as investment expenditure.

This view of expenditure on education has been adopted in this study. As regards, however, expenditure on health, the method described in the respective section in this chapter has been applied.

43. E. J. Mishan, *The Economic Growth Debate—An Assessment,* London, Allen & Unwin, 1977, pp. 40-41.

44. See Table 14, in Burkhard Strumpel's, "Higher Education and Economic Behavior," in *A Degree and What Else?,* ed. S. B. Withey, New York, McGraw-Hill, 1971, p. 57.

45. The fact that the more educated a person is, the more possibilities there are for his using a safety belt when driving, either for himself or for his family, is typical of the peculiar mentality acquired according to the level of education. This may mean, perhaps, that more educated people attach greater importance to human life than less educated ones (Strumpel, *ibid.,* p. 74).

46. See notes 42 and 43.

47. Strumpel, *op. cit.,* pp. 55-77.

48. *Reshaping the International Order, op. cit.,* p. 73.

49. A constant 5 per cent per year on the initial value of stock is estimated.

50. F. M. Fisher, Z. Griliches, and C. Kaysen, "The Costs of Automobile Model Changes since 1949," *The Journal of Political Economy,* Vol. LXX, (October 1962).

51. These 365 days include vacations and holidays. Still, during these days the family continues to need food, personal care, etc. During vacations, household needs are met by the market, e.g. food, hotels, washing and

ironing in dry-cleaning stores, etc. (such services are dealt with in the section on durables).

52. We have noted the objections to the use of the real average wage rate for non market activities which, if entering the market, would inevitably affect labour remuneration. This rate, however, is used here, as in other relevant studies (Tobin and Nordhaus, etc.), since it is not possible to assess all factors which might affect labour pay ("Is Growth Obsolete?", *op. cit.,* pp. 509-64).

53. On the basis of 1950 magnitudes, the productivity of services offered by restaurants, laundries, etc., has been estimated to be five times more than that of the respective services supplied by housewives or paid domestics. However, it has to be pointed out that it would be more correct to evaluate rising productivity over time, had it been possible to obtain the corresponding values without making arbitrary assumptions. In this case the rate of increase of the EAW-index would be lower than that depicted in Table 23.

54. On this subject, T. Scitovsky *(Papers on Welfare and Growth,* London, Allen & Unwin, 1964, pp. 213-14) remarks that the working week in U.S. industry became 20 per cent shorter over half a century (1909–1956), having declined from 51 hours in 1909 to 40.5 hours in 1956. He remarks, though, that these increases do not denote a rise of leisure time *per capita,* since the number of working women and of moonlighting persons increased. There was also another factor to be considered, which was not particularly evident in the 1960s, namely time lost in commuting to and from work, especially in large urban areas.

55. "To speak of nonworking time as a noneconomic use of time is symptomatic. The very term free time suggests a failure to realize that consumption time is a scarce commodity." (Staffan B. Linder, *The Harried Leisure Class,* New York, Columbia University Press, 1970, p. 7.)

56. To the degree that time is an economic good, the consequences of fluctuations in its prices are analysed — as for all economic goods — into an income effect and a substitution effect. As the price of working time goes up and people get richer, the income effect leads to higher demand for leisure time which is then considered to be a luxury good; it follows that such demand rises together with income. On the other hand, according to the substitution effect and the fact that the good "time" is now more expensive, there is a decline in the demand for leisure time. The outcome,

i.e., whether demand for leisure time will go up or down, depends on the relative power of these opposite forces.

57. Positional goods are those that "attract an increasing proportion of family expenditure as family income rises. Prominent examples are expenditures on education, vacation, housing, and a variety of personal services." (Hirsch, *op. cit.*, p. 28.)

The following table shows the relative priority of needs related to positional goods, at given income increases. It should be noted that, among six categories of goods, demand for leisure time comes last but one.

Income elasticity of demand, United States, 1960

	Percentage increase in consumption with 1 per cent increase in income
All goods	0.9
All services	1.1
Leisure	1.3
Education	1.6
Travel	1.4
Food away from home	1.2
(Owned vacation home)	(3.3)
(Lodging out of town)	(3.1)

As regards the competition of social status, Hirsch remarks: "The intensified positional competition involves an increase in needs for the individual, in the sense that additional resources are required to achieve a given level of welfare. In the positional sector, individuals chase each other's tails. The race gets longer for the same prize." (*Ibid.*, p. 67.)

58. Concerning the nature of leisure time, the following remark is made: "To the extent that time is the final good — daydreaming, lounging, resting — then the conservative interpretation is indicated. But if leisure time is one among several inputs into a consumption process, then it may well have been augmented by technological progress embodied in the complementary inputs — television, boats, cars, sports equipment, etc. (Tobin and Nordhaus, *Economic Growth*, Fiftieth Anniversary Colloquium V, New York, National Bureau of Economic Research, 1972, p. 42).

59. J. P. Robinson and P. E. Converse, *66 Basic Tables of Time Budget Research Data for the United States*, University of Michigan, Survey Research Center, 1967.

60. "Is Growth Obsolete?", *op. cit.*

61. *Social Indicators 1976,* Table, 10/1, p. 509.

62. Economic Report of the President, U.S. Government Printing Office, Washington, D.C., January 1979, p. 224.

63. U.S. Department of Commerce, Bureau of the Census, Statistical Abstract of the United States, 1978, p. 402.

64. Economic Report of the President, U.S. Government Printing Office, Washington, D. C., January 1979, p. 216.

65. *Social Indicators III,* Table 11/13, p. 559.

66. *Social Indicators III,* Table 11/13, p. 559.

67. In fact, the prevailing problems seem to be alarming on an international scale. As put forward by the authors of *The Global 2000 Report to the President*, "environment, resource and population stresses are intensifying and will increasingly determine the quality of human life on our planet... If present trends continue, the world in 2000 will be more crowded, more polluted, less stable ecologically and more vulnerable to disruption than the world we live in now."

CHAPTER FOUR

QUALITY OF LIFE INDICATORS

I. GENERAL REMARKS

The object of the previous chapter was to construct an index of economic welfare (the EAW-index), by estimating specific values for a number of variables which derive from national accounts data.

It will, however, be recalled from the analysis in the introductory chapter, that the notion of "total social welfare" comprises several different aspects, only one of which is strictly "economic". To be able to evaluate the effects of economic growth on the well-being of individual members of society, one must therefore examine also the direction of change in the non-economic or qualitative aspects of social welfare.

To avoid misunderstandings, it must be emphasised that what is argued here is not that only affluent societies are related to environmental (physical and social) degradation, resource depletion, social and subjective alienation, rising crime rates etc., for these things were known to earlier societies of scarcity and privation. All that is argued is that modern technological civilisation augments and aggravates the evils that already existed during different periods in history, to the point of rendering them extremely acute.

As far as environmental degradation is concerned, it is interesting to quote Plato, who wrote circa 400 B.C. that "...there are mountains (in Attica, Greece) which can now keep nothing more than bees but which were clothed

not so very long ago with fine trees... the annual supply of
rainfall was not then lost, as it is at present, through being
allowed to flow over a denuded surface to the sea..."
(*Critias*, 111 b-d).

There are numerous historical examples pointing to
the fact that environmental problems existed centuries before the emergence of technological industrialism. A well-
known instance is the collapse of the Mesopotamian civilisation caused by the destruction of the irrigation canals
supplying water from the rivers Tigris and Euphrates and
the ultimate saturation of the valley's fertile soil with salt. At
a much later time, in the 1700s, the quality of air in London
was probably worse than what it was in the early 1950s.[1]

Broadly speaking, some forms of environmental degradation, such as water pollution, are more pronounced
in poor countries than what they are in rich ones. The
reason is that the former cannot afford the means required
for the proper treatment of the water supply and other pollution media.

This brief survey seems to suggest that environmental and, in a more general sense, quality-of-life problems
cannot easily be attributed to any single cause, including
intensive industrialisation. Problems of this kind existed in
the past and will probably continue to belabour humanity
in the future. Hence, regardless of the specific reasons for
environmental degradation in different phases of human
history, modern technological industrialism has aggravated
the situation to such a degree that quality-of-life considerations have become crucial. Environmental problems grew
at a slow pace in the past; today, they are deteriorating at
alarming rates. What was once the concern of a few isolated
communities is now turning into a universal issue, not only
at the level of ecological survival but also as regards everyday living conditions and individual well-being.[2]

The preceding observations are not intended to acquit advanced industrialism of responsibility for the present plights of human existence. Given that this system possesses an abundance of both material goods and know-how in comparison with the severe scarcities and privations of the past, it bears a high degree of responsibility, for it can afford the means and the knowledge required to cope with such problems.

Increasing concern with quality-of-life problems indicates modern man's desire to live in a society that would permit him better to enjoy the fruits of his toil and to be in harmony both with himself and with his natural environment.

So long as the determinants of the quality of life remain relatively constant, as in the stages preceding affluence, changes in the level of total social welfare are more or less proportionately related to changes in the index of economic growth, according to the functional relationship assumed to exist between the two variables. Above a certain level of economic growth, however, when the various "symptoms" of affluence begin to appear, any further rise in the growth index has a direct bearing on the determinants of the quality of life, so that the functional relationship between economic growth and social welfare is modified to the extent that the latter may lose some of its momentum and may eventually decline.[3]

The activation of the factors that degrade the quality of life disrupts equilibrium at the margin among the different components of total social welfare, which can be economic, cultural, political, moral, psychological, etc. By contrast, in the classic line of argument, each of these components must yield equal marginal utility if a state of overall equilibrium is to be maintained.

More specifically, at the present stage of economic growth

in rich countries, whether total social welfare will improve or decline will depend on the relationship among the marginal utilities of the various components of total marginal social welfare. Thus, if the marginal increase in the economic aspects of welfare is less than the corresponding marginal degradation of the quality of life, the resulting marginal change in overall social welfare will be negative.

The deterioration in the quality of life is the outcome of the unqualified process of capital accumulation. As was stated earlier, entrepreneurship was given a specific meaning by classical economists, according to whose theories individuals were free to pursue their own advantage independently, since their success was assumed to contribute positively to society as a whole. The "new" world and "new" wealth seemed to justify a limitless effort for perpetual economic growth.

In recent times, however, it has become apparent that the discord between human efforts and equilibrium, in relation both to nature and to the individual's psyche, might lead to a breach, with unpredictable consequences for the human species. Mankind is becoming aware of the fact that, with a given technological potential, it has come close to the limits of the earth's stock of energy and wealth. Beyond these limits, the effects of inexorable laws of nature, such as the entropy law, will be highly intensified. The symptoms of this perilous trend are reflected in the deteriorating quality of life, given that the "human economy" is merely a subset of the physical world.[4]

The belief that man's well-being seems to depend on a constantly increasing flow of goods, widens the gap between today's compulsive behaviour and the principle of rational behaviour, which envisages a state of equilibrium. Yet the mode of behaviour, in affluent societies, cannot possibly have been based on the individual's independent choice; it must have been imposed by the expansionary institutional and market mechanisms of contemporary industrial states.

The views expressed here are deeply rooted in classical philosophical thought. When Aristotle referred to economic matters, it was always in relation to the well-being of society as a whole. While according to Solon the desire for wealth is unlimited, Aristotle maintained that material goods are merely a prerequisite for survival. Moreover, according to Aristotelian reasoning, human wants are in no way infinite, while scarcity is not regarded as a natural law; on the contrary, it derives from a mistaken conception of well-being, which relates everything to the acquisition of material wealth. Consequently, in Aristotle's opinion, a sound philosophy of life, together with well-managed institutions concerning the distribution of goods, overrides the law of scarcity. At the same time, it affords all the free time needed by the individual to exercise his supreme rights as a citizen.[5]

The hypothesis that higher income does not necessarily mean greater well-being for society as a whole was tested against specific social indicators referring to the overall quality of life. Such indicators can be either of an objective or of a subjective nature, although more often the two are mutually interrelated. In general, objective indicators refer to magnitudes such as income per head, population mobility, mortality rates, degree of equality of income distribution, educational attainments, or to phenomena such as crime, alcoholism, divorces, suicides, etc., whose increasing rates of occurrence can be attributed to the "neurotic" way of life in contemporary industrial societies. Subjective indicators on the other hand are based on perceptional evaluation, as expressed mainly in various social surveys or opinion polls. Although the validity of perceptional indicators has often been challenged, they are used as a means to supplement and attach a human dimension to the more or less "colourless" objective indicators.

II. SUBJECTIVE INDICATORS

One of the principal reasons for the seemingly loose relationship between income and happiness is the *revolution of rising expectations,* which is widely witnessed in today's consumer societies. This phenomenon may be attributed to a vicious circle which seems to be inherent in the relationship between production and consumption. For it must be pointed out that the revolution of expectations, typical of affluent societies, refers mainly to population groups that are relatively better off and not to those at the lower end of the income scale, whose expectations of an improvement in their lot would be fully justified.

The rapid obsolescence of consumer durables, as a result of — among other things — suggestive advertising, induces a virtually insatiable desire for "new" products. The implication is that the socio-economic system generates "potential consumption" which swiftly turns any pleasure gained from the possession and use of certain goods into discontent, owing to their rapid, more or less artificial, obsolescence.[6]

Thus the assumption that economic growth and the market mechanism are sufficient for the attainment of an optimum in terms of economic welfare is invalidated by the permanent shifting of expectations. Those of the members of a community who have just experienced an improvement in economic welfare enter directly into a phase in which they look forward to a further rise in income, regarding the previous rise as a thing of the past. This sequence is self-propagating *ad infinitum* and produces a dynamically mobile and constantly shifting geometric locus of social optima.[7] At the same time, the consumer's material well-being is no longer determined by the absolute amount of his income, but by his relative position on the income scale. According to the relative income hypothesis, consumers are compelled to demand not what is going to satisfy their wants, but rather what will maintain or perhaps even improve their relative socio-economic position. The orthodox rule that the income elasticity of demand for necessities is low while that for luxury goods is higher than unity is no longer valid. This is because the notions of "necessity" and "luxury good" become highly interchangeable over time, both among countries at a different level of development and within one and the same country at different stages of development. For instance, personal hygiene might be regarded as a luxury in an underdeveloped country, but it is a necessity in a developed one. Advertising and modern marketing techniques further distort the notions of "necessity" and "luxury", as well as the income elasticity of demand for the respective goods. To quote but one well-known example, demand for cigarettes is inelastic, although cigarettes are not a necessity.

Changes observed in poverty norms are indicative of alterations that take place over time in the relative position of individuals on the income scale. In the United States, for example, 47 per cent of the aged who constitute 10 per cent of the population come under the classification of poor, while the corresponding percentage for the entire population is 17 per cent.[8] This divergence is largely due to the different poverty norms used today and thirty or forty years ago. At that time, today's aged, who were not poor then, allocated their income between present and future consumption. Thus, forty years ago they started saving some of their income in order to maintain their standard of living at the same level for the rest of their life. The rapid changes that have taken place in the meantime, namely, the upward shift in the standard of living, have lowered their relative income to such a level that they are now classified as destitute.

In modern consumer societies, competition for the purpose of survival has given way to much keener competition
for the acquisition of positional goods. The latter are intended to ensure an improvement in the relative position of
individuals on the socio-economic scale. What is described
at the macroeconomic level as "growth-mania" corresponds
at the microeconomic level to the "income-mania" of consumers and to their insatiable "appetite" for positional
goods.[9]

Consequent upon this new kind of rivalry, the individual finds himself under constant pressure which diminishes his overall sense of well-being. The resulting reduction
in overall social welfare is the qualitative, psychological syndrome of the quantifiable aspects of welfare (i.e. the apparent
obsolescence of consumer durables, suggestive advertising
of "new" products, etc.) previously discussed.

The revolution of expectations has an obvious bearing
on fashion, product variety, advertising, etc., which are a
constant source of want creation, while at the same time
they lead consumers to discard their possessions before they
actually become obsolete. Equally obvious are the consequences of the relative income hypothesis. This hypothesis
makes individual satisfaction a function not only of a person's own level of income or consumption but also of the
corresponding levels of other members of a community. This
can explain in part why income increases do not lead to
analogous increments in social welfare. An individual may
have gained a rise in his absolute level of income, but if
everybody else's income rises in the same proportion, he
finally finds himself in an unchanged relative position on the
income-consumption ladder.

There are quite a number of social surveys, which point
to the particular relationship existing between income and
happiness.

The outcome of such surveys, considered in isolation, is often inconclusive. As has been pointed out, "some surveys indicate that the connection between basic economic factors and perceived quality of life is pretty loose and ambiguous; others show it to be close and clear".[10] This relationship is straightforward in within-country, cross-section comparisons, where the higher one gets on the income ladder, the most probable it is for him to belong to the category of "very happy" people.[11] Similar results were obtained for the year 1970 from a survey conducted by the American Institute of Public Opinion (AIPO), where the proportion of "very happy" Americans ranged from 29 per cent for the lowest income group questioned to 49-56 per cent for those in the highest income brackets.[12]

From other surveys of the same institute, which tried to classify the "not very happy" segments of the population among different income groups in a time-series from 1946 to 1970, the results obtained were similar to those previously mentioned: the percentage of "not very happy" people was higher for the poor than for the wealthier groups.[13]

However, these findings need not be generalised as universal tendencies. Other social surveys, probably making use of alternative methods of estimation, conclude that there seems to be no "clear linear relationship between either age or income and general life satisfaction".[14]

As one moves to international comparisons which do not rank the "happiness" scores of various income groups, but rather countries of alternative levels of per capita income according to overall percentage of population happiness, the relationship between income and happiness becomes less clear. Thus, in a tabulation of internationally comparable data based on World Survey III (1965), Britain scored first with 53 per cent of its sampling population classifying themselves as very happy, while it ranked third in per

capita income. The happiness scores for the United States,
W. Germany, France and Italy were 49, 20, 12 and 11 per
cent respectively. These countries ranked in the following
order regarding per capita income: first, the United States
with $2,790; second, W. Germany with $1,860; third, Britain
with $1,777; fourth, France with $1,663 and fifth, Italy with
$1,077.[15] These findings point to the loose relationship
existing between income level and degree of happiness. For
instance, Italy with 60 per cent of British per capita GNP
scored only 20 per cent of the respective British score of
population happiness. Similarly, while the United States
had 57 per cent higher per capita income than Britain, the
sampling happiness score of the former was 8 per cent lower
than that of the latter country.[16]

Nevertheless, beyond the above-mentioned within-
country and international cross-section comparisons, what
is of special interest in the context of the present essay is
the performance of time-series data; or, the way population
happiness scores, as revealed by specific social surveys in
economically advanced countries, change in the process of
further economic growth.

These perceptions are summarised in a number of
national surveys, which cover the period 1957-1978. These
surveys were made by the Institute for Social Research
of the University of Michigan. They demonstrate that the
proportion of very happy Americans — irrespective of the
income ladder — decreased from 35 per cent in 1957 to 30
per cent in 1978.[17] Characteristic in this respect is the fact that,
although during this period family income in absolute terms
increased sharply, differences in the percentages of "very
happy" respondents between income groups decreased;
thus, the 1957 differences which were pretty marked
almost levelled off in 1978. This was mainly because the
upper income groups' percentage of "very happy" people

converged towards that of the lower income groups: the percentage of the highest quartile fell from 47 to 32, that of the second from 41 to 32, and of the third from 34 to 27 per cent; however, the lowest income quartile of the population showed a slight increase in the rather limited proportion of "very happy" responses, which from 22 per cent in 1957 rose to 25 per cent in 1978.[18] Regarding the age distribution of perceived happiness responses, it is interesting to note that between 1957 and 1978 the decline in the proportion of "very happy" was more pronounced for the younger income groups. Thus, for those aged 20-29 the proportion of "very happy" fell from 40 per cent in 1957 to 29 per cent in 1978, for those in the 30-39 age group from 41 to 31 per cent, for those aged 40-49 from 33 to 31 per cent and for those in their fifties from 35 to 26 per cent. For the age group 60 and over there was an increase from 25 to 31 per cent.[19] Similar tendencies were observed in different educational groups, where the percentage of "very happy" responses decreased diachronically, the higher the educational level achieved. For example, while the percentage of "very happy" responses from those who did not attend high school increased from 23 to 28 per cent, it decreased for the "some high school" category from 30 to 25 per cent, for the high school graduates from 46 to 28 per cent, for the "some college" group from 43 to 33 per cent and for college graduates from 44 to 33 per cent.[20]

To sum up the above findings, it is interesting to note that the decline in the percentage of very happy responses has been confined mostly: *(i)* to the highest income groups, *(ii)* to the youngest population segments, and *(iii)* to those more educated among the population. These findings may imply that as material needs are met, people begin to aspire to the fulfilment of cultural and spiritual wants. Furthermore, regarding the age and educational-level distribution of happiness, the picture depicted may imply that the younger and the more educated one is, the less materialistic and the more aware of problems relating to the overall qualitative aspects of life one is apt to be.

There are several other studies which, by using time-series data, verify the tendency of a fall in the happiness scores of the American population in recent years. AIPO polls for the years 1946-1970 reveal that the percentage distribution of "very happy" Americans increased from 39 per cent in 1946 to 53 per cent in 1956. But from that year onwards, a gradual annual decline in the above magnitude led to 43 per cent of all Americans questioned classifying themselves as "very happy" in 1970. These findings are general, i.e. they do not apply to any particular income group, but to overall population samples.[21]

A similar tendency is revealed by National Opinion Research Center (NORC) polls, though the period examined is shorter. Thus, an already low — compared to AIPO poll figures — 35 per cent of "very happy" Americans in 1957 fell to 30 per cent in 1965. AIPO polls again, held for different income groups in the years 1963 and 1970, conclude that for all classes the proportion of very happy people fell from 47 to 38 per cent. Nevertheless, the decrease was more pronounced in the lower than in the higher income groups.[22]

Interesting in this respect are the findings of at least two national surveys made in 1972-1973, which are presented in a study by F. Andrews and S. B. Withey.[23]

In the first of these surveys, when Americans were asked to compare their life now (at the time the survey was made) to their life five years ago, 32 per cent answered that life had remained the same; another 30 per cent had noticed that life was getting worse; for the remaining 38 per cent who saw an improvement, the majority (24 per cent) stated that their life was getting "slightly better", another 10 per cent thought it was getting "somewhat better", and only 4 per cent rated their present life as "much better". Similar conclusions were reached in a survey covering 1971 and 1978, which suggested that life in the United States was deteriorating for 35 per cent of the sample (36 per cent in 1971), while the ratio of "worse/better" replies was 2.1 for both 1971 and 1978.[24]

Furthermore, other social surveys suggest that the proportion of "very satisfied" individuals is negatively correlated with the size of the city they live in, ranging from 20 per cent for downtown districts to 48 per cent for rural areas.[25]

The above-discussed findings of social surveys and opinion polls do not lead to clear-cut conclusions. They provide, however, some evidence to support the hypothesis of income relativity and growing expectations.

To the extent permitted by their reliability, the results of social surveys would appear to corroborate the common life experience of stress and discontent that has come to possess man in today's consumer society. The state of anxiety can be viewed otherwise as the psychological residual of the harm done to the physical and social environment. No one doubts the fact that the psychic cost of city life is much higher than the estimated damage cost due to heavy air pollution, bad traffic conditions, low standards of sanitation and sewage disposal facilities, etc. As stated elsewhere in this essay, damage cost is reckoned as the financial outlay required to "repair" only part of the harm suffered by the physical environment or of the constantly deteriorating conditions of urban life. Obviously, such an assessment of damage cost grossly underestimates the actual harm done to our surroundings and can be no more than a vague indicator of the stress and discontent which attend the continuous deterioration of the quality of life.[26]

III. OBJECTIVE INDICATORS

The following analysis concerns a number of objective indicators, which also serve to identify the problems
posed by further economic and industrial growth for human
happiness. Such evidence does not of course imply that
whatever positive effects economic growth may have on living
conditions, such as the rise in longevity, the improvement in
human health, the drop in illiteracy, better housing conditions and so forth, should be overlooked.[27] Nonetheless, the
main question raised in this essay refers to societies at a
very high level of economic growth, beyond which the cost
of any further improvement in the quality of life may actually be greater than the benefits that may be gained from such
an improvement. Indicators which lend further support to
the views advocated in this essay may conveniently be brought
under the general heading of "indices of social discontent".

The hypothesis that beyond a certain point the quality
of life is unrelated to a rise in income is confirmed by the
findings of a number of studies.[28] Such studies rank each
of the fifty states of the United States according to its score
in terms of "quality-of-life" (QOL) indicators. Among these
studies, one is based on U.S. "national goals", as expressed
in 1960 by the President's Commission on National Goals.
Another study uses "criteria of social well-being", which are
broadly classified as components of socio-economic well-being,
of social pathology and of mental health; in another study,
each state is ranked according to how much its QOL score
differs from the U.S. norm, using as indicators equality, living
conditions, economic status, education, health and welfare, etc.

Quality of life as expressed in the above-mentioned indicators does not exhibit a systematic positive relationship
to per capita income. Only for the 10 lower income states
quality of life seemed to be lower than for the richer 40.

For the latter states, with per capita income ranging from $2,500 to about $3,900 (1970 data), QOL rankings were diffuse, widely dispersed and clearly not reflecting any congruence between economic and social well-being. Thus, for the greatest majority of states, high per capita income is a weak proxy for social well-being.[29]

What is more important, is the very low correlation coefficient between income ranking and the top ten state rankings with respect to quality-of-life indicators found in all four relevant studies. Thus, the respective correlation coefficients range from 0.31 to 0.02. However, the opposite is not true; that is, for the lowest 10 states with respect to money income, the corresponding correlation coefficients in the four studies were 0.61, 0.75, 0.81 and 0.83.[30] This verifies the assumption already made that after a satisfactory level of income is achieved, there is no clear relationship between economic status and quality of life. Nevertheless, before this minimum income level is achieved, there seems to be a close relationship between poverty and bad quality-of-life conditions.[31]

In this study, an effort has been made to correlate a number of such indices with the process of economic growth. It has to be accepted of course that correlation does not necessarily imply causation. It has nonetheless been sought to establish some sort of indicative causal relationship between the evolution of an affluent community and some selected indices of social discontent (see Tables 25, 26, 27). For this purpose, the linear trend for the early sixties has been computed with regard to those variables for which time series were available. The extrapolation of this trend into the sixties and seventies has given the extent of the deviation between actual and fitted values. Accordingly, it has been found, for example, that the number of homicide victims per 100,000 population of U.S. cities had actually risen from 5.3 in 1950 to 9.2 in 1977, whereas the fitted value computed for the latter year on the basis of the 1950-1960 trend was only 3.3. The fact that the actual number of homicide victims in 1977 was almost three times higher than it would have been if the past trend had continued, seems to suggest the existence or activation of certain determining factors in modern consumer society.

Similar conclusions have been reached with regard to other related variables, such as the rate of violent crimes committed per 100,000 population, the actual value of which in 1977 was about 50 per cent higher than the corresponding trend value. Another equally interesting variable, for which statistical evidence is available for a sufficient number of years in the past, is the divorce rate per 1,000 population, which also shows a significant deviation between actual and fitted values. In 1977, for example, the actual value of the divorce rate was almost four times as high as the corresponding trend value (5.1 against 1.3).[32]

The only criterion taken into account in the selection of such indices has been the availability of sufficiently long time series. These indices give general support to the view that modern consumer societies generate factors which aggravate social discontent and lead to a proliferation of expressions of antisocial behaviour. On the presumption that a causal — however indirect — relationship does indeed exist between economic growth and the indices of social discontent, it has seemed worthwhile to examine in more detail three rather important aspects of the quality of life in affluent communities, namely crime, physical health and mental health.

1. Crime

Foremost among the various indices of social discontent and perhaps the one least subject to dispute is that

TABLE 25

Homicide Victims per 100,000 Population

Year	Actual values	Fitted values
1950	5.3	5.1
1951	4.9	5.0
1952	5.2	5.0
1953	4.8	4.9
1954	4.8	4.8
1955	4.5	4.8
1956	4.6	4.7
1957	4.5	4.6
1958	4.5	4.6
1959	4.6	4.5
1960	4.7	4.4
1961	4.7	4.4
1962	4.8	4.3
1963	4.9	4.2
1964	5.1	4.2
1965	5.5	4.1
1966	5.9	4.1
1967	6.8	4.0
1968	7.4	3.9
1969	7.7	3.9
1970	8.3	3.8
1971	9.1	3.7
1972	9.4	3.7
1973	9.8	3.6
1974	10.2	3.5
1975	10.0	3.5
1976	9.1	3.4
1977	9.2	3.3

Sources: U.S. Department of Commerce, Bureau of the Census, Statistical Abstract of the United States, 1979, p. 181. Historical Statistics of the United States, Colonial Times to 1970, series H 971-986.

TABLE 26

Violent Crimes per 100,000 Population

Year	Actual values	Fitted values
1957	117.0	114.2
1958	121.0	124.6
1959	126.0	135.1
1960	161.0	145.5
1961	158.0	156.0
1962	162.0	166.4
1963	168.0	176.9
1964	191.0	187.3
1965	200.0	197.8
1966	220.0	208.3
1967	253.0	218.7
1968	298.0	229.2
1969	329.0	239.6
1970	364.0	250.1
1971	396.0	260.5
1972	401.0	271.0
1973	417.0	281.4
1974	461.0	291.9
1975	482.0	302.3
1976	460.0	312.8
1977	467.0	323.2

Sources: U.S. Department of Commerce, Bureau of the Census, Statistical Abstract of the United States 1978, p. 177. U.S. Department of Commerce, Bureau of the Census, Social Indicators, 1976, p. 247. Historical Statistics of the United States, Colonial Times to 1970, series H 952-961.

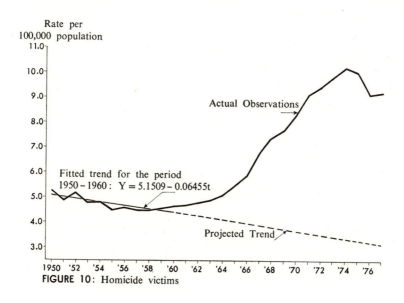

Rate per
100,000 population

Fitted trend for the period
1950 – 1960 : Y = 5.1509 – 0.06455t

Actual Observations

Projected Trend

FIGURE 10: Homicide victims

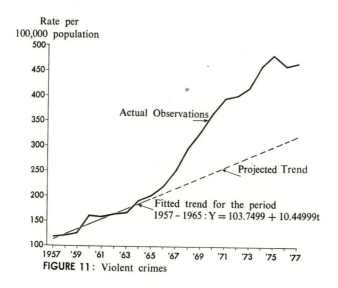

Rate per
100,000 population

Actual Observations

Projected Trend

Fitted trend for the period
1957 – 1965 : Y = 103.7499 + 10.44999t

FIGURE 11: Violent crimes

TABLE 27

Divorces per 1,000 Population

Year	Actual values	Fitted values
1950	2.6	2.6
1951	2.5	2.5
1952	2.5	2.5
1953	2.5	2.4
1954	2.4	2.4
1955	2.3	2.3
1956	2.3	2.3
1957	2.2	2.3
1958	2.1	2.2
1959	2.2	2.2
1960	2.2	2.1
1961	2.3	2.1
1962	2.2	2.0
1963	2.4	2.0
1964	2.4	1.9
1965	2.5	1.9
1966	2.5	1.8
1967	2.6	1.8
1968	2.9	1.7
1969	3.2	1.7
1970	3.5	1.7
1971	3.7	1.6
1972	4.1	1.6
1973	4.4	1.5
1974	4.6	1.5
1975	4.9	1.4
1976	5.0	1.4
1977	5.1	1.3

Sources : U.S. Department of Commerce, Bureau of the Census, Statistical
Abstract of the United States, 1979. Historical Statistics of the
United States, Colonial Times to 1970, Series B 216-220.

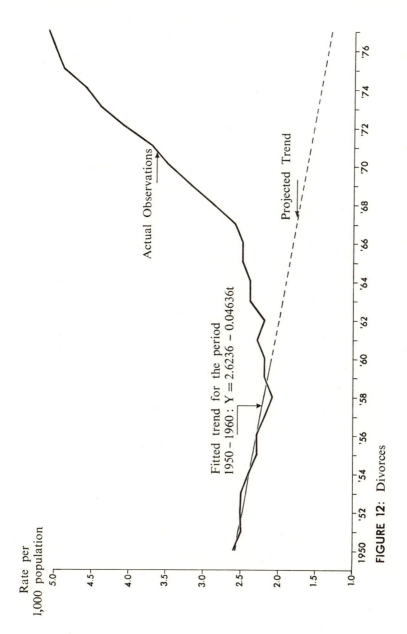

Rate per
1,000 population

Actual Observations

Projected Trend

Fitted trend for the period
1950 – 1960 : Y = 2.6236 – 0.04636t

FIGURE 12: Divorces

suggesting rapidly rising crime rates, which are more pronounced in advanced industrial societies.[33] For there can be
no doubt that nothing is so conducive to social welfare as
the feeling of personal security and freedom of movement and that nothing destroys that feeling so thoroughly
as crime.

Typical of the state of insecurity prevailing in major U.S.
cities is the total number of firearms sold each year to private
citizens, which rose from 2 million in 1960 to 7 million in
1974. On the wholly unrealistic assumption that the stock of
weapons in private hands was nil in 1960, it can be inferred
that, by the end of 1974, it must have reached a grand
total of 65 million pieces. This implies that about one in every
two American adults (precisely 42.5 per cent of the adult
population of 153 million in 1974) owned and perhaps carried a gun. Considering that the useful life span of firearms
is quite long, a more realistic assumption regarding the stock
of hand weapons in 1960 would lead to the conclusion that
the proportion of "gun-toting" citizens in the United States
is very much higher.[34] Furthermore, the Federal Bureau
of Investigation has estimated that one in every 550 U.S.
citizens is likely to fall victim to an assault.[35] It must of
course be remembered that high crime rates, drug addiction
and the other problems of urban centres are not confined
only to U.S. cities; analogous phenomena are found in
metropolitan areas of other industrialised countries, too. The
major reason for using examples drawn from American experience is the comparative abundance and accuracy of
statistical material available for that country.

It is a well-known fact that crime is very "expensive".
As a rough approximation only, it is worth mentioning that
in 1965 it was estimated that the amount of future income
lost by people who died of violence totalled $1.5 billion.[36]
The rise in the crime rate has been particularly impressive

over the last fifteen to twenty years. With specific regard to the four major categories of violent crimes, their number in the United States rose from 161 per 100,000 population in 1960 to 467 in 1977, while crimes against property increased from 1,726 per 100,000 population in 1960 to 4,588 in 1977.[37,38,39]

The strong relationship existing between economic growth and urbanisation on the one hand and the crime rate on the other is highlighted by the fact that, although the U.S. national average for offences against persons in 1974 was 33 per 1,000 population, the figure was close to 50 for metropolitan areas with a population of more than half a million people. In non-metropolitan areas, the corresponding figure was as low as 22. Thefts also show a tendency to increase with city size.[40] Another major factor bearing on criminality is relative poverty, which has come to rate as an equally (or even more) powerful factor as absolute poverty in the reduction of social welfare below what should be achievable today. For instance, black American ghettos have higher crime rates than "white" slum areas, owing to psychological and social reasons and to the fact that, as a group, blacks generally earn less than whites. Thus, according to a survey in five different parts of Chicago, the incidence of assaults in black ghettos was 35 times greater than in high-income districts.[41]

The implication is that, unless economic growth is combined with qualitative improvements, it fails to alleviate social problems and, in a broader sense, to enhance social welfare. It seems, from the evidence, that the relatively greater income disparities which often come in the wake of economic growth virtually force the weaker members of the community to find an outlet for their frustrations in crime and drug abuse.

Organised crime as well as so-called corporation crimes

involving the sale of illegal goods and services, e.g. narcotics or intoxicants during the days of the Prohibition, are obviously associated with the social and cultural traits of a community. Although accurate data are lacking, it would appear that the "business turnover" of organised crime is enormous. It is estimated, for instance, that illegal betting alone absorbed between $7 billion and $50 billion annually in the late sixties, at a time when the U.S. foreign aid budget was less than $2 billion.[42]

The growing social discontent owing to ever-rising crime rates is depicted in a series of social surveys. According to one of them, between 1965 and 1977 the proportion of persons afraid to walk alone at night rose from 35 per cent to 45 per cent. Furthermore, the percentage of those responding that criminals are not punished by the courts "harshly enough" rose from 57 per cent in 1965 to 88 per cent in 1977.[43],[44] In the same vein, between 1972 and 1975, those in favour of capital punishment were around 60 per cent of the respective sample, while over 70 per cent favoured the use of firearms in self-defence.[45] These and similar magnitudes must not simply be viewed as typical of the American way of life; they should be regarded as more or less typical of the majority of big cities round the world. What they seem to suggest is that the modern city dweller is gradually turning into a frightened creature, ready to make use of legal or even illegal forms of violence to defend himself against what he perceives as the growing aggressiveness of his fellow human beings.

Although these figures are impressive by any criterion, they are but a dim reflection of the actual situation. The financial cost of criminality is certainly far below its social cost in terms of the stress and fear caused by criminal offences. Fear, growing distrust and the dehumanisation of relations among individuals, represent the enormous, albeit unquantifiable, effective cost of urbanisation induced by industrial overdevelopment in the advanced economies.

The existence of conditions which have a growing negative effect on social welfare is also suggested by a number of other objective indicators coming under the general heading of "civilisation's diseases".

2. Physical Health

Despite the overconsumption of "health goods" in today's affluent societies, life expectancy in industrialised countries rose at a rather low rate over the last twenty years. Thus, the expectation of life at birth of a male in the United States grew from 65.6 years in 1950 to 66.7 in 1960 and 69.0 in 1976. The respective figures are 70.3, 71.2 and 72.1 for Sweden, 70.6, 71.4 and 71.5 for the Netherlands, and 69.8, 70.3 and 70.9 for Denmark.[46] Yet it cannot be argued that longevity has reached its biological limit.

The fact that infant mortality rates have dropped considerably in the economically advanced countries does not mean that public health conditions have improved for the entire span of human life. Thus, one in every three persons who have survived until the age of fifty dies of cancer, another one of cardio-vascular diseases, and only the third can expect to reach ripe old age. So, while life expectancy has increased, longevity has not, at least not commensurately.[47] Acute diseases of the past — mostly epidemics — have given way to no less serious chronic illnesses, which are primarily due to the way of life in contemporary society and to the harmful effects of industrialisation, such as spreading environmental pollution.[48] Cardio-vascular diseases are commonly regarded as having their origin in affluence, for they are caused mainly by overeating, lack of sufficient physical exercise and, generally, the kind of life one

is forced to lead in modern cities. The fight against arteriosclerosis begins virtually at birth and the outcome depends
on the diet followed throughout a person's lifetime. In a
survey concerning persons aged 34–44 in twenty-three industrial countries, the European Health Council came to the
conclusion that "malnutrition" was responsible for a 55 per
cent rise in the mortality rate for cardio-vascular diseases
over the last ten years.[49] Apart from overeating, excessive
consumption of alcoholic liquors and cigarettes also leads to
serious organic damage.[50]

It is important to stress that a strong correlation has
been established between heart disease and per capita income, as well as between death rates and overnutrition.
Thus the correlation coefficient between the death rate and
certain nutritional factors, such as the intake of calories,
fatty substances etc., ranges from 0.70 to 0.80.[51] According
to the American Heart Association, arteriosclerosis and other
diseases caused by an unhealthy diet cost the U.S. economy
tens of billions of dollars annually.[52] Regarding the United
Kingdom, it has been found that related diseases result in
the loss of 387,000 years of working life annually.[53] It would
thus appear that a very rich diet and the other concomitants
of affluence (mental stress, smoking, lack of physical exercise)
are strongly and positively correlated with the incidence of
cardio-vascular diseases.

The discussion will again turn to the example of the
United States and the health conditions of its population, in
conjunction with the fact that expenditure on health in that
country is among the highest in the world. Thus, as a proportion of disposable income, U.S. expenditure on health
rose from 5.9 per cent in 1965 to 8.8 per cent in 1977. At
1950 prices, national health expenditure rose at an annual
rate of 4.9 per cent between 1950 and 1977.[54] On a per
capita basis, U.S. health outlays rose from $240 in 1960

to $450 in 1975 (at 1972 prices).[55] Also, the United States spends more on biomedical research than any other country. Contrary to the expansionary trend in expenditure, however, public health indices have improved rather slowly since 1960. In fact, disparities in health expenditure among advanced countries seem to have a negligible effect on mortality rates, life expectancy, etc.[56] This means that the marginal contribution of health expenditure to the improvement of health conditions is very close to zero for countries with approximately the same standard of living.[57] Despite enormous expenditure on health, data for the mid-1970s indicate that the United States had a rather mediocre performance in terms of most vital statistics (life expectancy, infant mortality, etc.).[58,59] According to one view, an additional explanation for this might be that the country is faced with the problem of uneven distribution of health services and with the profit-seeking character of the sector. To the extent that health becomes a luxury good, the cost of the industry rises, while the overall quality of services rendered falls.[60]

Furthermore, as in other sectors of the U.S. economy, in the health sector also it is not always "wants" that create "goods", but "goods" — in this instance, hospitals and doctors — that generate "wants".[61] Although this kind of argument is rather out of place where matters of health are involved, it implies nevertheless a systematically irrational behaviour on the part of consumers, regardless of whether demand is related to motor cars or antibiotics.[62]

Despite the enormous amounts spent, public health in the United States is not so high as one could expect, especially in comparison with the corresponding performance of other countries. This might be due to the way of life prevailing in the United States as in other industrial nations, together with increasing environmental pollution in major urban centres, which generates unforeseeable hazards for human health. The stress caused by living in a highly competitive society, the loneliness and monotony of life in large cities, the lack of proper physical exercise, unhealthy eating habits, excessive reliance on canned and preserved foodstuffs, smoking, drug abuse, air and water pollution, and even "noise pollution" have probably played a decisive role in neutralising the favourable effects which would otherwise have come from large-scale spending on medical care. It thus appears that a considerable part of the funds spent in the sector of health is used to remedy the harmful effects of modern city life. To the extent that this happens, health expenditure must be regarded as "corrective" and not as being directly conducive to the enhancement of social welfare.[63]

3. Mental Health

What has just been discussed concerning public health in general applies also to mental health, where the role of the contemporary neurotic way of life is prominent. As has been argued, some forms of serious mental disorder exhibit the highest frequency among people living in downtown areas. Characteristic in this respect is the spectacular increase in the total number of care episodes in mental hospitals etc. between 1955 and 1975, which rose from 1,700,000 to 6,400,000. Over the same period, the proportion of in-patients in the total number of people being attended to decreased from 77 per cent to 28 per cent. The opposite, however, is true for out-patients, whose share in the total rose from 23 per cent in 1955 to 72 per cent in 1975.[64]

Here it is worth mentioning that "the total cost to industry of all forms of stress-related illness and other manifestations, a large slice of which can be attributed directly or indirectly to the working environment, must be enormous, beyond the scope of most cost accountants to begin to calculate. Some scientists estimate that it may represent in the order of 1–3 per cent of GNP in the United States".[65]

The lack of psychic equilibrium typical primarily of the urban way of life is indirectly reflected in the rising divorce rates found in major urban centres. For the whole of the U.S.A., the number of divorces and annulments rose from 390,000 in 1953 to 977,000 in 1974. The number of divorced women aged 14–44 (per 1,000 women) rose from 15 in 1957-1959 to 32 in 1972-1974. The social impact of such a situation relates directly to the total number of children involved, which rose from 330,000 in 1953 to 1,099,000 in 1974.[66] The number of divorces seems to be positively related not only to the degree of urbanisation but also to labour and social mobility and the population explosion in a given area. For example, in the western United States, where social mobility is twice as high as in the northeast, the number of divorces is four times higher.[67]

Experts have already termed this way of life the "new immediacy". Unfortunately, this hedonistic philosophy, given the intense feeling of loneliness attending it, fails to enhance personal happiness. On the contrary, it reduces happiness and leads people to violence and self-destruction.[68]

Besides high crime rates, a further consequence of the impersonal way of life offered in metropolitan areas and in cities with high social mobility is the increase in alcoholism and drug abuse. In New York, for instance, alcoholics are three times as many as in North Dakota, while the number of Californians who die of cirrhosis of the liver is twice as high as the U.S. national average. In the United States as well as in other countries, drug abuse seems to have reached the proportions of an epidemic, despite doubtful and scarcely reliable statistics. According to a number of surveys, the proportion of school-children who admit to having used or to being regular users of soft drugs (marihuana) ranges from 50 to 85 per cent. The National Narcotics Institute reported that marihuana users increased by 5 per cent in 1976, compared with 1975.[69] Drug abuse is very often the symptom of a social disease and may be interpreted as an act of protest against the materialistic and unspiritual values of affluent society.

To conclude this discussion of indicators pointing to growing social discontent and the deteriorating quality of life in affluent communities, it should be mentioned that the cultural interests of modern man seem to have lost a great deal of their originality in recent years. The point has been reached where an overwhelming majority of people prefer to watch television instead of engaging in other intellectually stimulating activities. In fact, the proportion of those who reported reading as their best leisure activity dropped from 21 per cent in 1938 to 14 per cent in 1974. Similarly, cinema and theatre attendance dropped from 17 per cent in 1938 to 9 per cent in 1974, dancing from 12 to 4 per cent and listening to the radio from 9 to 5 per cent. By contrast, television viewing rose from 28 per cent in 1960 to 46 per cent in 1974.[70]

The figures just given may appear to be less significant, compared to the more impressive data concerning the "catastrophic" effects of pollution and environmental degradation on those human communities where unrestrained growth has become the dominant way of life. Nevertheless, they provide further important evidence that "civilised" man risks the gradual minimisation of his normal reaction and resistance to the growing challenge of our times. The above discussion does not exhaust the subject; there are numerous other factors negatively affecting social welfare. Considering them all, however, is beyond the scope and purview of the present essay.

IV. GENERAL CONCLUSIONS

This essay centres round the effects of economic growth on human welfare. It distinguishes between the purely economic aspects of welfare — items susceptible to quantification — and the non-economic aspects of it, which are not directly susceptible to quantification but are reflected in quality-of-life indicators.

As far as the purely economic aspects of welfare are concerned, it appears that cost variables increase faster than the positive elements of economic welfare. On the assumption that no parametric changes will occur in the meantime, the EAW-index — now rising at a diminishing rate — will reach a point of bliss in about thirty years. Beyond that point, increases in the national product will be unable to improve economic welfare, unless a breakthrough leading to a new technology, free of side-effects, takes place.

The analysis would be incomplete if it did not include the non-economic social aspects of human welfare, which, together with the economic ones, determine overall human well-being. Chapter four presents facts and figures which have a direct bearing on the quality of life. The general impression conveyed by QOL indicators is that economic growth has already become a self-defeating effort.

It is believed that, if it were possible to construct a composite index, summarising the overall effects of economic growth on welfare — an exceedingly difficult task — the worsening situation would be more readily discernible. ·

As shown in the fourth chapter, modern man seems to be in a state of mental stress, which has adverse effects on personal well-being and social peace. Mental stress occurs partly owing to purely psychological factors, such as boredom or discontent, a side-effect of affluence and the lack of ideals, and partly as the acquisition of more and more material wealth becomes one's only purpose in life. To a considerable extent, however, discontent is due to objective factors, which make for the enormous and unquantifiable social cost of economic growth. The deterioration of the ecosystem, environmental pollution and the unfavourable living conditions in urban centres resulting in violence, crime, drug abuse etc., have a catalytic effect on the individual's peace of mind and his mental ability, in many advanced industrial societies. Besides, uncertainty regarding mankind's fate in the face of, among other problems, the persisting energy crisis leads in the same direction.

Thus, apart from the quantifiable aspects of pollution, urbanisation, and the accelerating depletion of the earth's stock of energy resources and other raw materials, there must be an enormous residual of unquantifiable damage in terms of the social cost involved in the overall deterioration of modern man's quality of life. This should have a direct negative impact on the ability of the individual to enjoy the material goods that are in such plentiful supply in consumer societies. The degradation of the quality of life is corroborated by various "indices of social discontent", based on statistical evidence of increases in criminal and terrorist acts, suicides, drug abuse, divorces etc. It should also be mentioned that, in recent years, cultural interests seem to have lost a great deal of their originality, as indicated by the growing preference for television viewing at the expense of other intellectually more stimulating pursuits.

The feeling of discontent seems to be widespread among members of affluent communities, as depicted in many social surveys. The conclusions of a recent survey made in the United States by the Harris organisation are typical in this respect. According to that survey, when Americans from all over the country were asked whether they favoured a continuation of the effort "to achieve a higher standard of living", only 17 per cent gave an affirmative answer, while 79 per cent replied that they would prefer to see "a campaign to inform the people how they can live better, having at their disposal the basic necessities of life." Apart from these replies, only 22 per cent expressed a preference for continuing research aimed at the construction of larger and more efficient mechanical systems, while 66 per cent voiced their preference for a more humanised way of life. Though such surveys and social indicators cannot substantiate the existence of a causal relationship between economic growth and social well-being, they nevertheless indicate that modern man seems to be in a constant state of anxiety regarding his very survival. This state of affairs is not of course confined to a single country; it applies equally to all affluent societies.

NOTES

TO CHAPTER FOUR

1. "...The Air of the City, especially in the Winter time, is rendred very unwholsome: For in case there be no Wind, and especially in Frosty Weather, the City is cover'd with a thick *Brovillard* or Cloud, ...so that the Inhabitants thereby suffer under a dead benumming Cold..." (Quoted from Timothy Nourse, *Campania Felix*, London, 1700, p. 352, in W. J. Baumol and W. E. Oates, *Economics, Environmental Policy and the Quality of Life*, Englewood Cliffs, N. J., Prentice-Hall, 1979, p. 15 — Original spelling retained.)

2. One of the fields where environmental degradation becomes particularly acute and difficult to solve is marine and especially ocean pollution. As mentioned in the "Global 2000 Report to the President": "Industrialization, which is heaviest in the Northern Hemisphere, is now introducing pollutants into the oceans in quantities which are beginning to cause significant deleterious effects on resources and the environment. The important coastal zones are being changed at ever increasing rates to the detriment of natural resource productivity."

"...The more important effects, however, stem from the largely unnoticed, and undetected, chronic low-level pollution. Because most pollutants fall in the latter category and do not generate public outcry, the general attitude is to consider the oceans as an important resource to be utilized in disposing of the wastes of man. This utilization requires the identification of substances that jeopardize marine resources and human health and the determination of acceptable levels — an extremely slow process because the pathways and effects are extremely complex and long-term. Demonstrable threats to marine resources are seldom available within time spans that could effectively stop the pollution prior to adverse accumulations." ("The Global 2000 Report to the President," U.S. Government Printing Office, Vol. Two, 1980, p. 111.)

3. Even if the actual practice of more modern methods — such as the "catastrophic theory" — were feasible, it is probable that this would have even more impressive results as regards the decline of total social welfare. In other words, if we accept the fact that, after a certain level of economic development, the deterioration of the quality of life at given increases of the rate of economic growth are not marginal but rapid, then it is inferred that the decline of total social welfare, owing to the deterioration of the quality of life caused by further economic growth, will also not be marginal but sub-

stantial. Which means, of course, that the concept of Paretian optimisation is automatically rejected. Even the actual use of the compensation criterion, with its concomitant problems, would not constitute a favourable element for economic growth. Because, evidently, in a state of radical, non marginal degradation, the losing members of society cannot be indemnified by the gaining ones since the marginal benefits of the latter from economic growth are lower than the damages incurred by the former owing to the deterioration of the quality of life.

The afore-mentioned shift of relative magnitudes from marginal to rapid changes is also held to be due to the fact that the magnitudes of the world economic-ecological system change at exponential rates. For instance, if a variable increases at a constant annual rate, say 7 per cent, its present value will have doubled by the end of a 10-year period. If the rate is 2 per cent, it will have doubled by the end of a 35-year period, and so on. In particular, experts claim that the exponential increases of world population and capital (despite the considerable differences between countries owing to unequal distribution) will eventually lead to the final catastrophe of the ecosystem. This is because the rate of increase in the various magnitudes is such as will not permit them to reach and stop at their natural limits, but, inevitably, cause them to exceed the safety margin into the final catastrophe. According to the same view, even if measures were now taken to reduce the expansion rate of population and capital accumulation, inherent delays in both the natural ageing of the population and the technological obsolescence of capital would cause an upsurge in these magnitudes for many years to come. Thus, even if world birth rates drop below the "substitution limit" — which is two children per couple — it has been estimated that world population will continue to increase for 70 years. *(The Limits to Growth,* A Report for the Club of Rome, New York, Universe Books, 1972, p. 145.)

4. Kenneth E. Boulding, "The Economics of the Coming Spaceship Earth," in *Toward a Steady-State Economy,* ed. H. Daly, San Francisco, Freeman, 1973, p. 123.

5. *Primitive, Archaic, and Modern Economies — Essays of Karl Polanyi,* ed. G. Dalton, Boston, Beacon Press, 1971, pp. 98-99.

6. J. K. Galbraith's "dependence effect" comes here into play, according to which needs are created not by the tight supply of a good but by the good itself.

7. The above are corroborated by various researches and soundings conducted in the United States from time to time. Thus, in a survey made by the

U.S. Survey Research Center, one of the questions asked over a period of years was whether there was any special expenditure surveyed persons would like to make. Both in the beginning of the 1950s and ten years later, 60 per cent of the answers given were affirmative and 30 per cent negative. That is to say, during 10 years of overconsumption not only the frequency of those having unsatisfied wants did not decrease, but also the list of desirable goods augmented. Curiously enough, those who stated they had no unsatisfied wants were mainly poor or aged people. That is to say, the percentage of negative answers declined with the increase in income and rose with age.

In particular, only 16 per cent of persons under 35 years of age in 1962 stated they had no unsatisfied wants, whereas the corresponding percentage for persons over 65 years of age was 53 per cent. The percentage of persons with an annual income of under $3,000 who stated they had no unsatisfied wants was 43 per cent, whereas the corresponding percentage for persons with an annual income of over $10,000 was 25 per cent.

The percentage of affirmative answers dropped from 61 per cent in 1962 to 56 per cent in 1968 and 51 per cent in 1971. It should be noted, however, that 1971 was a recession year. The fact that the number of persons with high income having unsatisfied wants declined considerably during the period of recession is indicative of the relationship between "the mentality of expectations" and economic conjuncture — income breeds new expectations for additional income. (George Katona, *Psychological Economics*, New York, Elsevier, 1976, pp. 156-57.)

8. Tibor Scitovsky, *The Joyless Economy*, New York, Oxford University Press, 1976, p. 117.

9. As family income increases, positional goods and services absorb an increasing share of family expenses. Take for instance private expenditure on education, a house in the suburbs and a host of personal services (Fred Hirsch, *Social Limits to Growth,* Cambridge, Mass., Harvard University Press, 1976, p. 28; also Table on p. 29). The increasing material product raises the demand for positional goods; it is a demand, however, which can be satisfied in few cases only. Increasing competition for positional goods triggers increasing personal needs as even more resources are needed to attain a given level of welfare. The individual is cast into a vicious circle; struggle becomes longer whereas results remain the same (Hirsch, *ibid.,* p. 67).

10. Elemér Hankiss, "Structural Variables in Cross-Cultural Research on the Quality of Life," in *The Quality of Life — Comparative Studies*, eds. Alexander Szalai and Frank Andrews, International Sociological Association/ISA, 1980, p. 48.

11. *Ibid.,* Table 4, p. 50.

12. Richard Easterlin, "Does Economic Growth Improve the Human Lot? — Some Empirical Evidence," in *Nations and Households in Economic Growth*, Essays in Honor of Moses Abramovitz, eds. P. David and M. Reder, New York, Academic Press, 1974, Table 2, p. 100.

13. *Ibid.,* Table 3, p. 100.

14. Bernard Blishen and Tom Atkinson, "Anglophone and Francophone Differences in Perceptions of the Quality of Life in Canada," in *The Quality of Life, op. cit.,* Table 1, pp. 29-30.

15. R. Easterlin, *op. cit.,* Table 7, p. 107.

16. On an international basis, the findings of a Gallup Opinion Index examining the economic expectations between 1977 and 1980 among ten countries showed the U.S.A. first with the largest rise in the proportion of those believing that the economy would worsen (U.S.A.: from 54 to 79 per cent; Japan: from 30 to 40; Canada: from 53 to 70; Switzerland: from 45 to 53; Australia: from 54 to 60). By contrast, in the Federal Republic of Germany and in the Netherlands there was a decrease (from 40 to 27 per cent and from 57 to 42 respectively), while in the United Kingdom there was practically no change. (*Social Indicators III,* [December 1980], Table L. Economic Expectations, Selected Countries: 1977 and 1980, p. LX.)

The result of such surveys is that both on a cross-country and on a diachronic within-country basis, there seems to be no clear relationship between financial situation and expectations for a better future.

17. Angus Campbell, *The Sense of Well-Being in America,* McGraw-Hill, 1981, p. 29.

18. *Ibid.,* Appendix Table 4, p. 241.

19. *Ibid.,* Appendix Table 9, p. 245.

20. *Ibid.,* Appendix Table 5, p. 242.

21. R. Easterlin, *op. cit.,* Table 8, p. 109.

22. R. Easterlin, *op. cit.,* Tables 8 and 10, pp. 109 and 111.

23. F. Andrews and S. B. Withey, *Social Indicators of Well-Being,* New York, Plenum Press, 1976, p. 315, exhibit 10.4.

24. *Social Indicators III,* (December 1980), Table K. Evaluation of Life in the United States: 1971 and 1978, p. LX.

25. *Metropolitan America in Perspective,* eds. A. H. Hawley and V. P. Rock, Table 7.7 : Percentage Distributions of Respondents in the Quality of Life. Study: Level of Community Satisfaction for People in Communities of Different Sizes, p. 438.

26. The importance of environmental quality in a general sense — from clean air considerations to housing conditions — over and above the quantifiable dimensions of the problem discussed in chapter three, is recognised as one of the most serious hazards of modern life: "... we are concerned with our physical surroundings: with the air we breathe, the water we use, the housing we occupy, the landscapes we see, and the transportation systems and urban patterns that determine the spatial dimensions of our lives." (U.S. Department of Health, Education, and Welfare, *Toward a Social Report,* Introd. by W. J. Cohen, Ann Arbor, University of Michigan Press, 1970, p. 27.)

Thus how can one remunerate the social cost to an economy whose industrial production is going to grow at, say, 4.5 per cent per year and which, in the absence of any major technological breakthrough, is about to have four times as much pollution as it now has by the end of the century and ten times the present level by 2020? "This hypothetical projection alerts us to the fact that a new type of natural resource scarcity is emerging." *(Ibid.,* p. 28.)

Or what can one say about urban quality and social well-being when of the six major U.S. cities for which data exist none meets "even the tentative short range standards..."? *(Ibid.,* p. 30.) What amount of damage cost can be set for the contamination of major rivers and waterways which is projected to double by 2020, unless "we raised the effectiveness of all treatment to 95 per cent... but 95 per cent treatment goes to the outer limits of present technology, and would perhaps triple or quadruple treatment costs"? *(Ibid.,* pp. 32-33.) Furthermore, how can we account for the fact that "...6 million Americans are subjected to hazardous noise levels at their jobs"? (*Ibid.,* p. 34.)

27. Such data, however, may sometimes be mere indicators of the phenomenon they are supposed to reflect. On educational achievement, for instance, Robert D. Mare observes that although educational levels have increased enormously during the twentieth century, performance on standardized aptitude and achievement tests for high school students has declined dramatically since 1963. This decline is due partly, according to Robert D. Mare (pp. 107-109), to changes in school curricula. "In the early 1970s," he states, "there was evidence of a shift from traditional academic coursework to a broader array of elective subjects. At the same time, there was little evidence of a corresponding erosion at the elementary level. Since the bulk of the tests

for which the score declines are observed measure more complex academic skills, the apparent curriculum change at the advanced grades away from traditional academic courses may well explain some of the trend'' (p. 108). He admits, however, that his interpretation "rests on meagre evidence.'' The issues to be investigated include "how actual course content has changed, which students are taking the new electives, and how other schooling trends — grade inflation, increased absenteeism and relaxation of standards — interact with shifts in curriculum.'' (Robert D. Mare, Trends in Schooling: Demography, Performance, and Organization, *The Annals of the American Academy of Political and Social Science*, January 1981, pp. 96-122.)

28. J. Wilson, *The Quality of Life in America*, Kansas City, Midwest Research Institute, 1967; D. Smith, *The Geography of Social Well-Being in the United States: An Introduction to Territorial Social Indicators*, New York, McGraw-Hill, 1973; Ben-Chieh Liu, *The Quality of Life in the United States, 1970: Index, Rating, and Statistics*, Kansas City, Midwest Research Institute, 1973.

The first of these studies is based on U.S. "National Goals'' as expressed in 1960 by the President's Commission on National Goals.

The second (Smith's) is based on "criteria of social well-being'' as expressed through certain groups of variables, such as the variables of socio-economic well-being, of social pathology and mental health.

Lastly, Liu's study ranks each State according to its variation from the U.S. Norm, while the variables used are similar to those of the first two studies.

With few exceptions, rankings are remarkably similar across all studies and stable over time, although QOL is defined differently.

29. Although each of these studies differs from the others in the definition and measurement of the quality of life, there seem to be no major differences in their respective ranking. Thus, as Ben-Chieh Liu points out, the ranking of his study has a correlation coefficient which is 0.84 as compared to Smith's study, 0.78 to Wilson's and 0.73 as compared to the study in *Lifestyle Magazine* (Ben-Chieh Liu, "Variations in the Quality of Life in the United States by State, 1970,'' *Review of Social Economy*, Vol. XXXII, [October 1974], No. 2, p. 139).

30. *Ibid.*, pp. 140-41.

31. In a more recent study of his, Liu points out that "...policies focusing on economic growth alone do not concomitantly guarantee the betterment of other quality-of-life concerns, especially the deteriorated environmental

quality which might have partially resulted from the growth." The finding of a negative correlation coefficient of -0.12 between economic and environmental indexes, makes Liu wonder how it would be possible "to enrich other important quality-of-life components, while aiming at economic growth." (Ben-Chieh Liu, "Economic and Non-Economic Quality of Life: Empirical Indicators and Policy Implications for Large Standard Metropolitan Areas," *The American Journal of Economics and Sociology,* Vol. 36, [July 1977], No. 3, pp. 233-34.)

32. See Tables 25, 26 and 27 in this book.

33. Two diametrically opposed theories have been formulated concerning the impact of the economic factor on crime. According to the first one, advocated by Xenophon, Plato, Virgil, Thomas Aquinas, Thomas More, the French philosophers of the enlightenment and others, the reason for criminality should be sought in poverty: people steal because they are poor. Consequently, an increase in well-being will eliminate or at least reduce crime. The second theory, put forward in the 19th century by the Italian Filippo Poletti, attributes criminality to well-being. According to Poletti, the more economic and social progress leads to an increase in commercial transactions and interpersonal contacts, the more opportunities for crime multiply. This view has been criticised mainly by those who refuse to accept that such a high price as growing opportunities for crime has to be paid for the achievements a society is particularly proud of (obviously meaning economic progress). According to Leon Radzinowicz and Joan King (*The Growth of Crime,* Pelican Books, 1977), "yet psychological research, as well as experience, offers plenty of evidence that this can be the case" (p. 93).

34. *Social Indicators 1976,* Table 6/16. Annual Production and Imports of Firearms for Private Sale: 1960-1974, p. 252.

35. Just before the assassination attempt on 30 March 1981, President Reagan had appealed to the national conference of the building and construction trades unions for support for his economic programme and deplored the increase in violent crime which, he said, was "making neighborhood streets unsafe and families fearful in their homes" *(International Herald Tribune,* April 1, 1981).

36. David M. Gordon, *Problems in Political Economy: An Urban Perspective,* Lexington, Mass., Heath & Co., 1971, p. 287.

37. *Social Indicators III,* (December 1980), Table 5/6, p. 241.

38. *Ibid.,* Table 5/7, p. 242.

39. Interesting is the fact that, on an international comparison among sixteen countries, the United States came first with the largest number of deaths due to homicides per 100,000 population. This rate rose from 7.7 in 1970 to 10.0 in 1975. The corresponding rate for the second country was only 2.6 deaths in 1974 *(ibid.,* Table 5/20, p. 252).

40. *Social Indicators 1976,* Table 6/7, p. 248.

41. D. M. Gordon, *op. cit.,* p. 289.

42. D. M. Gordon, *op. cit.,* p. 295.

43. *Social Indicators III,* Table 5/1, p. 237.

44. *Ibid.,* Table 5/2, p. 237.

45. *Social Indicators 1976,* Table 6/18, p. 253.

46. *Social Indicators III,* Table 2/11, p. 96, and U.N., *Demographic Yearbook,* 1956, 1960.

Quality of Life Indicators, Selected Countries

Country	Infant Mortality Rates, 1977 (per 1,000 live births)	Life Expectancy at Birth (years)	
		Male	Female
Canada	14.3	69.34[1]	76.36[1]
Denmark	8.9	70.9[2]	76.5[2]
France	11.4	69.0[3]	76.9[3]
Germany	15.5	68.3[4]	74.81[4]
Japan	8.9	72.15[2]	77.35[2]
Netherlands	9.5	71.5[2]	78.0[2]
Sweden	8.0	72.12[2]	77.9[2]
Switzerland	10.7	70.29[5]	76.22[5]
United Kingdom	14.0	69.8[2]	75.8[2]
United States	14.0	69.0[2]	76.7[2]

[1] Period 1970-1972.

[2] 1976.

[3] 1974.

[4] Period 1974-1976.

[5] Period 1968-1973.

Sources : OECD, *Manpower and Social Affairs Committee, Inventory of Data Sources for Social Indicators,* January 1979; U.N., *Demographic Yearbook,* 1976, and *Statistical Yearbook,* 1978.

47. Michel Remy, *L'homme en péril,* Editions Stock, 1971, p. 64. According to the same author, centenarians are much harder to come by today than what seems to have been the case one or two hundred years ago.

48. The pollution of the seas causes an upsurge of epidemic diseases (polio, hepatitis, encephalitis) which, however, special drugs help prevent or cure. There are even new diseases whose outbreak is clearly due to industrial pollution. In Japan, for instance, we have the Minamata disease, caused by eating fish and crustaceans poisoned with methylmercury, a by-product of the polyvinyl industry, and the Itai-Itai disease caused by water pollution with cadmium in the ore-extracting industry. These two diseases have caused many deaths and left many people severely handicapped. It should be noted that they first made their appearance in Japan where economic development without qualitative specification is unparalleled. Industrial pollution causes not only the outbreak of new diseases but also the increasing recurrence of known ones. It has been proved that DDT is absorbed by plants and is cancer-inducing. Cancer of the stomach is also caused by the appearance in water of large quantities of nitrate. A whole series of chemical substances used in industry have been proved to be cancer-conducive: asbestos used in ship-building, quarries and the construction and car industries; arsenic used in the chemical industry and by vine-growers for spraying; vinyl chloride used in the plastics industry, and radioactivity generated in pertinent production stations and military bases — to mention but a few. At the same time, food plays a prominent role in the spread of diseases. It has been proved that the addition of preservatives in foodstuffs is dangerous to health. The people of Iceland, Southern Germany and the Baltic seaports, who consume large quantities of smoked foodstuffs, are prone to intestinal cancer. The use of antibiotics in fish preservation causes severe allergical reactions. The amount of DDT present in foodstuffs — prior to its prohibition the average American consumed 0.1-0.2 mg. daily — is not rejected by body mechanisms; on the contrary, it is stored in the brain, the ovaries and other sensitive organs. *(Science et vie,* No. 117, December 1976, pp. 52-92 and *passim.)*

49. It is known that vegetable fats processed under high temperature (200° C.) cause cancer of the stomach. Yet, although a few years ago they were regarded as food "good for animals only", they are now produced and consumed in large quantities for reasons of economy (M. Remy, *op. cit.,* p. 72).

Bread, now "refined" in the form of white bread, has lost its nutritive value, and cereals, in general, by being so refined lose 50 to 90 per cent of their vitamins *(ibid.,* p. 84). Other foodstuffs now consumed in large quantities, such as refined sugar, alcohol, coffee, not only do not contribute any nutritive substances — although contributing a lot of calories — but also destroy the existing stock of vitamins and other valuable substances.

Having said enough on quality, let us briefly deal with the quantity of food consumed by modern man. People in rich countries consume more calories than needed; the difference between calories consumed and energy required is deposited in the body as fat. Recent research in French schools showed that the number of obese children increased during the last 10 years while 20 per cent of French adults are obese. Overconsumption by children of powdered milk (rich in fats) and starchy foods was lately witnessed. Bad nutrition in children and adults leads to increased possibilities that they will suffer from arteriosclerosis at a later age. In France, sugar consumption has risen from 16.6 kilos per person at the beginning of this century to 40 kilos today. Consumption of fatty substances has also increased. In W. Europe, the U.S.A. and Canada fats provide 40 per cent of total daily calories consumed. It is well known that fats and sugar raise the cholesterol content of blood, leading to cardiovascular diseases. Moreover, the drop in the consumption of fruit and vegetables leads to gastrointestinal disorders *(Science et vie, op. cit.,* p. 71).

50. In France, for instance, demand for intoxicants increased by 143.3 per cent between 1960 and 1974. Also, 8 to 9 per cent of the French high school population is very close to the limits of alcoholism. As regards smoking, one of the worst causes of heart disease and cancer, a 1974 study revealed that one in every two boys and one in every five girls in French high schools were regular smokers by the age of 18 *(ibid.,* p. 141).

51. Colin Blythe, "Problems of diet and affluence," *Food Policy,* Vol. 1 (February 1976), Table 1, p. 92.

52. *Ibid.,* p. 96.

53. *Ibid.,* p. 96. Registrar General's Annual Estimates of the Population of England and Wales and of Local Authority Areas, 1973-1974 (London, HMSO, 1975).

54. *Social Indicators III,* p. 58.

55. Some data concerning health expenditure in the U.S.A. appear in the table on the next page.

Total and Per Capita Health Expenditure

Year	Total health expenditure ($ billion) (at current prices)	Total health expenditure ($ billion) (at 1972 prices)	Total health expenditure as a percentage of GNP	Per capita health expenditure ($) (at 1972 prices)
1950	12.0	29.6	4.2	194
1960	25.9	43.4	5.1	240
1965	38.9	57.6	5.7	296
1970	69.2	76.0	7.0	371
1975	122.2	96.1	8.0	450

Source : U.S. Department of Commerce, Bureau of the Census, Statistical Abstract of the United States, 1978.

56. T. Scitovsky, *op. cit.,* p. 165.

57. If we accept the view that longevity is the main target of medicine, we must also accept the fact that pertinent expenditure has already reached or exceeded its saturation point. "The desire to live longer may be unsaturable, but to spend more money on health is not the way to its fulfillment." (T. Scitovsky, *op. cit.,* p. 165.)

58. In 1969, expenditure on health in the U.S.A. totalled $62 billion, having increased by 11 per cent over 1968 or doubled against 1960. Of the above amount, $6 billion was spent on the purchase of drugs, $10 billion on medical supplies and $35 billion on hospitals and nurseries (D. M. Gordon, *op. cit.,* p. 336).

59. T. Scitovsky, *op. cit.,* Table 7, p. 166.

60. These views are expressed in D. M. Gordon's "Problems in Political Economy: An Urban Perspective" (*op. cit.*). Though the data of that book belong mainly to the mid or late sixties, the trends depicted must in general hold. As, for instance, the fact that "...rising costs have served to widen the gap between the medical care available to the affluent and to the poor..." (p. 324) or that "...the industry spends... on advertising... twenty-five cents out of every sales dollar and more than three times as much as it spends on its much heralded research and development effort" (p. 338).

61. This is corroborated by the frequency of operations or hospital entries. It is interesting to note in this respect that higher frequency of operations among people living in a certain region compared with those living in other regions of the same state (e.g. Kansas) is related to the number of hospitals, surgeons and doctors in general. The more hospitals and doctors

there are in a certain region, the higher the percentage of people operated upon (T. Scitovsky, *op. cit.,* p. 168).

62. As regards antibiotics, it is estimated that their consumption in the U.S.A. is five times the real needs of that country. It is also estimated that 30,000 persons die annually from excessive or erroneous use of drugs, while an amount of $2.25 billion is spent to cure side-effects (T. Scitovsky, *op. cit.,* p. 169). It is also known that, according to a recent report by the World Health Organisation, only 200 basic drugs are necessary, compared with the thousands of proprietary medicines available on the world market.

63. The method of computing corrective health expenditure has been described in the chapter concerned with the compilation of the EAW-index, according to which the amount of expenditure entered in the index must be raised annually at a rate equal to 50 per cent of the increment of the per capita health outlay at constant prices. Regarding the QOL indicators discussed in the immediately preceding sections, it should be said that they attempt to express the psychological state of a population striving to remain healthy in the midst of an environment systematically threatening to destroy both its physical and its mental health.

64. *Social Indicators III,* Table 2/6, p. 93.

65. R. N. McMurray, "Mental Illness, Society's and Industry's Six Billion Dollar Burden." [1973: Reprinted in the Bulletin of the British Psychological Society, (February 1980).]

66. *Social Indicators 1976,* Table 2/9, p. 67.

Divorces, Selected Countries: 1977

Country	Rate per 1,000 population
Canada	2.4
Denmark	2.5
France	1.3
Germany	1.8
Japan	1.1
Netherlands	1.6
Sweden	2.5
Switzerland	1.5
United Kingdom	2.4
United States	5.1

Source : U. N., *Statistical Yearbook,* 1978.

67. In California, the state of divorces, 6 marriages out of 10 are dissolved. In Orange County (SW of Los Angeles), where population grew by 600 per cent within 13 years, this ratio was 8 to 10. In such areas "... there is a large, highly mobile, anonymous and fleeting crowd seeking new experiences and emotions, with no roots or family ties whatsoever" (C. E. Philips, American Institute of Family Planning, U.S. Office of Vital Statistics).

68. A 1969 survey made at Berkeley University, the main center of student riots, revealed that 36 per cent of students surveyed had no close friends. Many of them disclosed that they played a prominent role in these upheavals not for political or other reasons, but just to feel a sense of belonging to a team and the warmth of friendship through collective action.

69. Greek newspaper *Ta Nea*, and *Washington Post,* August 30, 1977.

70. *Social Indicators 1976,* Table 10/4, p. 511.

EPILOGUE

The principal inference from the foregoing analysis is that, over the last few decades, continuing economic growth in affluent societies has been accompanied by a diminishing rate of increase in social well-being, which tends to an absolute decline if past trends are extrapolated into the future. This is because "industrial man" has lost the sense of moderation and balance in life and has focused his attention on the unconstrained expansion of unqualified wealth. The Stoic teaching "ἀκολούθως τῆ φύσει ζῆν" (live in accordance with nature), which is identified with the highest good, happiness, is no longer adhered to.[1] This motto implies that to be happy "life must be in accord with our innate reason and with the general order of the world".[2]

Harmony between human life and the universe has been disrupted. Suffice it to mention in this respect that air pollution and other forms of environmental degradation are actually threatening to change even the climate of the earth. This would, of course, trigger a chain of reactions with unforeseeable effects on every life form on this planet; eventually, that could be thought of as man's penalisation for having ignored the eternal laws of nature and of the universe.

At the same time, however, man's inner harmony seems also to have been disrupted, since his works are at variance with his own spiritual and intellectual roots. As a result, mental stress, fear, aggressiveness and social apathy have become the principal characteristics of life in affluent societies.

The consequences of sustained growth in terms of material wealth for total well-being can only be assessed by considering the side-effects of economic growth on both the quantitative and the qualitative aspects of social welfare. The quantitative aspect of the problem may be summarised in the fact that, during the phase of rapid expansion, the industrial nations ignored the question of overall ecological equilibrium; they were particularly concerned with maximising economic growth and overlooked the cost inherent in this process, which could eventually cancel out or even reverse any benefits obtained from it. In this sense, the advanced countries of the world, including those which have developed according to a centrally planned model, have lived and are still living by consuming the ecosystem's stock of renewable and non-renewable resources, such as raw materials, energy sources, water, fresh air, natural beauty, fauna, marine life, etc.[3] At the same time, they are "consuming" mankind's humanistic heritage, since they have become involved in an endless and selfish struggle to acquire more and more goods. In this anti-humanistic, anti-cultural climate, a new "advanced" type of human being has been born, *homo neuroticus,* who is called upon to pay in terms of chronic stress for having chosen technological knowledge instead of age-old wisdom and unbridled utilitarianism instead of consummate beauty.

Mankind — particularly that part which is primarily responsible for the present situation — is faced with crucial choices, which may be summed up in the juxtaposition of certain important alternative solutions. Will economic growth be pursued indefinitely, at the expense and no doubt to the detriment of social welfare? Is the developed part of the world going to remain indifferent to the constantly increasing discrepancy between private and social cost, between present doubtful benefit and future probable catastrophe? Until recently, the rich nations had totally overlooked the normal limits of economic growth, perhaps because these limits were still considered remote or perhaps because technological progress could always push them back. Now, however, it is no longer possible to ignore the problems associated with economic growth; they must be dealt with drastically through an awakening of world conscience. If this happens, the prevailing situation of excessive material wants will give way to a balanced increase in material well-being and in social, cultural and aesthetic enjoyment.

The position taken in this essay is not antidevelopmental.[4] It is simply accepted that economic growth may improve social welfare only if the outcome of a careful cost-benefit analysis turns out to be in favour of social benefit. This implies that economic growth should not be regarded as an aim in itself; whether it should continue or not and at what rates depends not merely on a global examination of all related parameters, but mainly on the way in which economic growth shapes and affects the overall quality of life.

Most of the side-effects of economic growth relate to the quantitative aspect of social welfare and are associated with existing technology, with the present "state of the arts". This of course does not imply that technological progress is undesirable, for there can be no doubt that, in previous phases of development, it played an enormously important role in improving living and working conditions. Nor should it be overlooked that it can offer great services, particularly in the development of poverty-stricken regions. What must be changed and improved is the tendency of today's technology towards the wasteful use of scarce resources, and the bias in favour of magnification.

Incessant technological progress has produced an illusion among industrial nations, namely that the acquisition of constantly larger amounts of material wealth can continue for ever, together with a commensurable improvement in social welfare. This, however, would be tantamount to ignoring the side-effects of economic growth on the environment, on ecological equilibrium, and even on the individual's inner stability. The principal disadvantage of this mega-technology is that it is resource-abusing, polluting and destructive to the environment, with unforeseeable consequences for life on earth. Many of the negative aspects of technological progress spring largely from the fact that it originated mainly in the research laboratories of World War II and of the constantly expanding arms industry. It has therefore become biased in favour of a method of production outside the needs and dimensions of man.[5]

It is possible, however, that in the future a technological breakthrough will occur, one that will provide the basis for new and revolutionary improvements in anti-pollution devices, energy uses, production, distribution of goods, etc. According to this optimistic view, in the future all kinds of shortages in raw materials, energy etc. may be overcome by introducing methods that would make infinite substitutability feasible. Thus raw materials that are scarce or produce side-effects would be replaced by others that are in abundance and are free from ill effects. With specific reference to the vital sector of energy, experts consider it a virtual certainty that a "philosopher's stone" will be found one day in the form of perfected methods of capturing and converting unlimited energy flows, such as solar energy, into non-entropic, non-polluting energy sources. Experience shows that technological breakthroughs occur either in emergencies — such as wars — or in fields offering strong incentives for research — such as space technology, where spectacular progress has been made — or finally, when the balance of the biosphere and the very survival of man are at stake. If the present crisis, which is threatening the entire ecosystem and the human race with extinction, could induce revolutionary innovations, these could go a long way towards easing the crisis. If this happens, energy for instance will cease to be a menace and will become a source of unconstrained progress.

Meanwhile, apart from any accomplishment in the fields of production and of environmental conservation, what is really needed to increase the chances for a better life is a new approach. An approach which, among other things, would give technology a new and broader perspective in the sense of diverting it from material wealth maximisation to the purpose of maximising individual and social well-being. Thus, in the first technological revolution man used his common sense and everyday experience to combine his labour with the energy of coal and steam in order to improve his life; in the second, science in its most sophisticated form became a direct productive force; a third technological revolution should herald a return to the human scale. In this way, man would once more be reconciled with the actual dimensions of the ecosystem and with himself.

A word of caution is in order here concerning mainly the optimistic attitudes implicit in the above views. First of all, it should be stressed that a solution to the energy problem would not be a panacea for all the problems caused by technology. The reason is that use of the various energy substitutes existing today in plentiful supply, such as coal, is prohibitive owing to the high pollutant content of their residues. However, even if the energy problem is completely solved in the not too distant future, the crisis that has already broken out cannot be overcome over the next few decades.[6] This is because it takes time for a new form of energy to become widely used. So, the industrial countries have practically missed the chance to take advantage of a transitional "overlapping" period, marked by sufficient supply, rational use and predictable increases in the prices of energy sources.

Since it is widely admitted that the next few decades are going to be a time of crisis, every effort should be made to minimise the undesirable effects of past negligence. Especially in the production and marketing of goods, it is necessary to attain the highest possible rate of waste recycling and to seek the prolongation of the average life span of those goods which are now subject to very rapid technological obsolescence. Meanwhile, advertising should cease being suggestive and conducive to the general trend towards wastefulness and artificial obsolescence and should be called upon to play a more informative role. It is obvious that concerted action ought to be taken to "internalise" and re-assess the actual social cost of production, while economising as much as possible on conventional forms of energy until their full technological substitution is — if ever — achieved.

The new period which has just begun should be one of conservation, re-assessment and waiting, to give mankind time to reconsider its present set of priorities. The transition of affluent into post-industrial societies, which is already under way, would play an important part in overcoming the crisis. During the post-industrial phase, the most important role would be that of information and of the development of interpersonal services rather than of industrial technology. Besides, the incidence of consumer demand would shift from material goods, whose production is associated with the side-effects mentioned previously, to interpersonal services, especially those related to cultural and educational activities. In this framework, collective consumption would expand at the expense of private, egocentric consumption. The post-industrial society would be far removed from the postulates of the "puritan ethic", according to which only labour makes human existence meaningful and vindicates man's conduct as a useful member of society. By contrast, the post-industrial state would provide more leisure time, during which individuals would be able to foster their intellectual development thanks to cultural "goods" supplied by the system and to improve relations among themselves as active members of their group. They would thus cease leading the isolated, insatiable and antisocial life of today's consumer society.

Such developments could enable industrial societies, and with them the world as a whole, to pass with a minimum of losses through the crucial decades between now and the new era envisaged by those who take an optimistic view of the future achievements of mankind.

The foregoing are tangible problems, which are more or less closely related to the existing technological frontier. They do not, however, concern — at least not directly — that enormous segment of social cost which defies measurement and stems from the systematic deterioration of the quality of life in affluent societies. Above all, they have no bearing on psychic damage, which is constantly growing. Thus, stress and anxiety, together with environmental, aesthetic or other degradation, are a common experience in modern consumer societies, which are thought to be prospering by national income accounting standards. Another equally common experience is the growth of the protest movement, beyond the scope of narrow economic or class demands. All these phenomena are closely related to the dehumanisation of interpersonal relations, the alienation of modern man from his humanistic heritage, and the demolition of culture. Despite the anthropocentric aims of the industrial revolution, which assigned top priority to the happiness of the individual, modern industrial societies do not seem to have evolved in that direction. Their members are to some extent cut off from both the past and the future; they seem to have lapsed into apathy or to be unable to establish those values that would not only ensure mankind's biological presence on earth, but would also render it meaningful. The root cause of these undesirable symptoms lies in the fact that, even when seen in the light of crude utilitarianism, affluence seems to have failed to make the consumer prosperous and happier. Instead, the system has dethroned the individual and has replaced him with an exogenously given technology, which he cannot control. The affluent society seems to have defeated its own purpose of creating a true abundance of opportunities to develop the aptitudes of human beings.

Economic growth has not only proved futile, in its inability to secure greater prosperity for already advanced industrial societies, but has also failed to eradicate poverty in the Third World. The gap between rich and poor nations has in fact widened after World War II. This, no doubt, as far as the developing countries are concerned, can be partly attributed to sustained high birth rates, which have given rise to the fundamental issue of population control. However, the population explosion and other endogenous problems in these countries do not lessen the responsibilities of the developed part of the world. By using up most of the earth's finite stock of productive resources, the rich countries leave little room for hope that the inhabitants of the Third World will escape poverty. Mention should be made of the view that, for the poor countries to reach the 1970 level of the ten richer countries of the world in per capita stock of industrial metals, world output of such metals in that year would have to be sixty times as large.[7] The perpetuation of living conditions below subsistence level not only poses moral and humanistic problems for the industrially developed countries, but also remains a constant threat to world peace.

The implication is that, even by purely egocentric criteria

concerning the advisability of economic growth regardless of qualitative considerations, such growth is seen to be both irrational and futile. Some years ago, the specific growth model could have been accused of being ineffectual for the poor countries; today, it seems to have failed to operate properly even in the rich ones.[8]

Therefore, the need for a new economic and social order — one that would optimise economic growth only as a means of "maximising" social welfare — based on an awakening of world conscience is now more imperative than ever before. In this connection, W. Leontief points out that, to attain high growth rates, the developing countries need above all far-reaching social, political and institutional changes, while at the same time world economic order must be altered to a significant extent.[9] In this context, it is necessary to bridge the gap between the level of cultural development and technological civilisation founded on scientific knowledge. This, however, presupposes the re-education of peoples in the principles of humanism, irrespective of ideological, ethnological or other differences. Once it is agreed that the level of the quality of life in a society depends on educational attainment in the broadest sense of the word, training its members should once more become the Platonic "principle of utmost principles" (*Laws,* 765e).

It may be argued that technological and economic progress has created the material prerequisites for a qualitatively better society, one which by proper re-education will lead to a new order of humanistic aspirations. The influence exerted mainly on young people by changes in a society's value system, as reflected in its educational system, is evident. Every child comes into the world as a *tabula rasa,* with only its latent aptitudes and talents, to suffer progressively the disruptive influence of consumer society. Then, schooling at

all levels, instead of protecting the young individual against
all kinds of psychological compulsion, prepares him or her
for a more or less ambitious professional career. The fundamental task of education, which is to create responsible citizens, is thus overlooked. The educational system must therefore change, to enable schools in the broader sense to operate
as vehicles of the humanistic heritage, instead of remaining
merely reservoirs of accumulated scientific knowledge. Within
such a framework, humanity may become aware of the ideal
of true happiness and the terms on which it can be achieved.
These terms concern individual communities as well as the
entire world, and will help develop a sense of ecumenicity,
which may eventually lead to an age of peace and fulfilment.

All this requires proper care so that the citizen will not
be subjected to propaganda and brain-washing in the name
of re-education. It is only in the context of free choice that
individuals can operate rationally and responsibly; only
then will they be able to reject the classical motto which has
institutionalised egoism and extravagance and according to
which "private vices turn into public benefits". The modern
society of one-sided technological and scientist knowledge,
virtually a society of cultural indigence, should turn into
a society of wisdom. Thus man would recover his balance
with regard to both his inner self and the world around
him, while by living "in accordance with nature" he would
regain true happiness. The Platonic saying "the very rich
are not virtuous and those who are not virtuous are not
happy" (*Laws*, 743e) thus seems to remain as valid as ever.
Happy men, according to Plato, are those who live in due
measure and balance in a "healthy" society, in contrast to
the citizens of "soft" or "inflamed" states.[10] The characteristics of the Platonic inflamed society are similar to
those of modern consumer societies, which have far exceeded the normal limits of want creation and have been

afflicted with "consumption-mania" and extravagance.

The tenet of the "Golden Mean" in life, far removed from the quest for riches as a prerequisite of good living, is age-long and is found in deeply differentiated civilisations ranging from Classical Greece and the teachings of the Christian Church Fathers to the religious and social doctrines of Buddha and Confucius.[11]

As a matter of fact, anthropocentrism and the need to guide the individual towards a new philosophy of life and the state towards a new economic and social order are already taking the form of permanent social demands in the modern world.[12] Ordinary people claim the right to determine by themselves the content of their happiness and the quality of their life. This attitude has evolved into a peaceful uprising, which embodies not the demands of a specific class or ethnic group but the protest of millions of people oppressed by the bonds of poverty or the tyranny of meaningless affluence.

In conclusion, it should be said that this essay aims to contribute to an awakening of public conscience, to help arrive at a new economic and social order: then the rich industrial countries will re-orient their expansionary activities in order to secure a constantly rising level of social welfare based not on ever increasing quantitative magnitudes, but rather on the improvement of qualitative aspects.[13] At the same time, this will enable them to divert more resources to the poorer countries, so that the latter can achieve their objective of escaping from poverty and starvation.

These aims can only be attained when a philosophy of life based on new moral values prevails, so as to enable man to live in harmony with nature and with himself. Re-education, a prerequisite for the achievement of this objective, will free man from the tyranny of *toujours plus* and bring him closer to the attitude of "constantly better". Thus, human beings will have a chance to regain their lost happiness through spiritual and cultural rather than materialistic values, which will be in harmony with the true nature of man.

Summing up, it has to be stressed once more that economic growth should not be regarded as a good in itself but only as a means that would lead to an improvement of social well-being. In this sense, economic growth has to be sustained at the least possible social cost; it should continue without resource waste and environmental degradation; without resort to the distorting role of persuasive advertising and conspicuous consumption; without the debasement of social services and social values and the deterioration of city life. Furthermore, it should promote prosperity in terms of both more useful material goods and more and better collective services; it should progressively substitute public for private consumption and social interests for selfishness; and it should lead to greater cultural attainments. In sum, it should enhance social well-being not only materially but also in terms of individual happiness and social peace. Such a type of economic growth would then be warmly welcomed, as a necessary condition for ensuring the attainment of more of a better life.

NOTES

TO EPILOGUE

1. "And this is why the end may be defined as life in accordance with nature or, in other words, in accordance with our own human nature as well as that of the universe, a life in which we refrain from every action forbidden by the law common to all things, that is to say, the right reason which pervades all things" (Diogenes Laertius, *Lives of Eminent Philosophers*).

2. According to I. N. Theodoracopoulos, the saying "live in accordance with nature" signifies for Zeno of Citium the agreement of life with ourself, while for Cleanthis it signifies agreement with universal reason. These two views complement each other and sum up the Stoic philosophy. "...Virtue lies in a rational life, the agreement of life with innate reason and with the general order of the world." (I. N. Theodoracopoulos, *The Philosophy of Zeno*, Academy of Athens, Library of the Centre of Research and Greek Philosophy, pp. 251-52.)

3. It should be stressed that the same responsibility, though perhaps to a different degree, burdens the economies that have developed industrially according to the socialist model. The practical application of the notion that only work generates value has led even the socialist economies to waste natural resources and energy since, according to the above notion, natural resources, e.g. petroleum, have no other value than that imparted to them by human labour. In the same way, the destruction of the physical environment, air and water pollution etc. have been caused by the unqualified desire of the socialist economies to achieve their fastest possible industrial transformation.

4. According to the Sierra Club: there exists "no blind opposition to progress, but opposition to blind progress." (*The Limits to Growth*, A Report for the Club of Rome, New York, Universe Books, 1972, p. 154.)

5. The dependence of modern technology on the arms industry is evident, if it is borne in mind that research in this sector takes up more capital than the sectors of energy, health, education and food put together. The total of public expenditures on research and development in the sector of armaments amounts annually to nearly $30 billion and engages half a million scientists and engineers.

At an international level, annual expenditures for armaments exceed $400 billion. The share of the two superpowers exceeds 50 per cent, with a share of two-thirds in the world arms trade (*Development and the Arms Race,* an address by R. S. McNamara, University of Chicago, May 22, 1979).

6. Isaac Asimov has expressed an interesting view concerning the use of hydrogen fusion in producing energy. Although he believes that the world energy problem will be solved by this method, he notes that "...it may take as long as 30 years to translate that into large fusion power stations... It may well be 2020 then, before we are a fusion society. It will be wise to conserve oil supplies and to substitute other energy sources (coal, shale, wind, flowing water ...) to keep us going until fusion can take over. And we might also strive to develop solar energy, making use of the nuclear fusion power that already exists and that we call the sun" (I. Asimov's Zero Vision, in "40 Years Hydrogen Fusion Will Solve Energy Problems," *Science Digest,* September 1979).

7. See Harrison Brown, "Population Growth and Affluence: The Fissioning of Human Society," *Quarterly Journal of Economics,* May 1975.

8. "The charge against that order in the past was that it worked well for the affluent and against the poor. It cannot now even be said that it works well for the affluent. This is an additional incentive for evolving a new economic order..." (Kurt Waldheim, in *Reshaping the International Order,* A Report to the Club of Rome, New York, Dutton, 1976, p. 9.)

9. "To ensure accelerated development, two general conditions are necessary: first, far-reaching internal changes of a social, political and institutional character in the developing countries, and second, significant changes in the world economic order" (*The Future of the World Economy,* A United Nations Study by Wassily Leontief *et al.,* New York, Oxford University Press, 1977, p. 11).

10. The distinction between the moderate, "healthy" state and the irrational extravagance of the "inflamed" state is made by Plato in his *Republic* (372e, 373b, 373e).

11. Respect for nature is clearly seen in the obligation of all good Buddhists to plant a tree every few years and care for its growth (E. F. Schumacher, "Buddhist Economics," in *Toward a Steady-State Economy,* ed. H. Daly, San Francisco, Freeman, 1973, p. 236).

12. It seems that mankind's only hope lies in the universal acceptance of a philosophy founded on respect for life in the broadest possible sense, including respect for nature in all its aspects. For there can be no doubt

that affluent societies are to a large extent societies of destruction. Having been brought up in effect on antihumanistic and purely materialistic principles, they have fostered the creation of "consumer-man". This new type of human being, alienated from the microsystem of consumer society and alien — with catastrophic effects — to the ecosystem, remains a member of liberal society only in appearance. In actual fact, he is oppressed by various factors such as the manufactured wants of affluent societies and the dominant technology of the "megamachine". The only hope of weakening the oppressive influence exerted on people by consumer society lies in the awakening of the conscience of the ordinary man in the street. When this is done, the individual will cease to accept passively the rules of a game in which he takes no part and there will be room for a real improvement in his overall well-being.

"For many generations, so long as the inherited nature of God remained strong in them, they were submissive to the laws... and thus their wealth did not make them drunk with pride so that they lost control of themselves and went to ruin; rather, in their soberness of mind they clearly saw that all these good things are increased by general amity combined with virtue, whereas the eager pursuit and worship of these goods not only causes the goods themselves to diminish but makes virtue also to perish with them." (Plato, *Critias*, 120d - 121b, transl. by R. G. Bury, London, Heinemann, 1961.)

13. Economic theory has tended to neglect quality-of-life problems, not because economists have not been aware of them but because, as Assar Lindbeck points out, "...there has been a tendency for the externalities to slip down to the footnotes, particularly in our textbooks, and that social conditions have hardly been at the center of the analysis in economic textbooks." Lindbeck calls for a dynamic restatement of the Walrasian general equilibrium system, so that it can "be related to the ecological equilibrium system of our natural environment, as well as to the man-made environmental system." No doubt, such a restatement is urgently necessary. But first a lot of problems, both theoretical and practical (e.g. operationalisation of the new enlarged system), will have to be adequately dealt with. (Assar Lindbeck, *The Political Economy of the New Left*, 2nd ed., New York, Harper & Row, 1977, pp. 14-15.)

INDEX OF NAMES

Ahluwalia, M., 39
Andrews, F., 142, 166, 167
Aquinas, T., 170
Aristotle, 26, 135
Ashley, Sir William, 27
Asimov, I., 190
Atkinson, T., 167
Ayres, R. E., 123

Barnett, H., 116, 117
Baumol, W. J., 27, 119, 123, 164
Beckerman, W., 115
Bergson, A., 38
Blishen, B., 167
Blythe, C., 173
Boulding, K., 112, 113, 124, 165
Brown, H., 25, 190
Buddha, 187
Bury, R. G., 191

Campbell, A., 167
Chenery, H., 39
Cleanthis, 189
Cohen, W. J., 124, 168
Confucius, 187
Converse, P. E., 95, 128
Cooper, C. L., 25

Dalton, G., 165
Daly, H. E., 121, 165, 190

d'Arge, R., 123
David, P., 167
de Jouvenel, B., 26
Diogenes Laertius, 189

Easterlin, R., 167

Fisher, A. C., 117
Fisher, F. M., 126

Galbraith, J. K., 25, 165
Georgescu-Roegen, N., 121
Giarini, O., 25
Goeller, H. E., 121
Gordon, D. M., 170, 171, 174
Griliches, Z., 126

Habermas, J., 27
Hankiss, E., 166
Hawley, A. H., 168
Heal, G., 119
Herfindahl, O. C., 116
Hicks, J. R., 38, 42, 115
Hirsch, F., 41, 116, 128, 166
Holdren, J., 25
Hotelling, H., 118
Howe, C. W., 26

Juster, F. T., 113, 115, 124, 125

Kaldor, N., 42
Katona, G., 166
Kaysen, C., 126
Kendrick, J. W., 125
Keynes, J. M., 28, 54
King, J., 170
Kneese, A., 123
Kuznets, S., 39, 40

Leontief, W., 185, 190
Lindbeck, A., 191
Linder, S. B., 127
Little, I. M. D., 39
Liu, B.-C., 66, 67, 68, 123, 169, 170
Lovins, A., 120

Malinvaud, E., 112, 119, 122
Malthus, T. R., 27
Mare, R. D., 168, 169
Marshall, A., 28, 54, 118
McCulloch, 27
McMurray, R., N. 175
McNamara, R. S., 25, 26, 190
Mill, J. S., 6, 27, 28
Mishan, E. J., 126
Moore, W. E., 112
More, Sir Thomas, 170
Morse, C., 116, 117
Moss, M., 113
Myrdal, G., 112

Nath, S. K., 38
Nordhaus, W. D., 53, 95, 113, 114, 115, 117, 119, 122, 124, 125, 127, 128
Nourse, T., 164

Oates, W. E., 27, 119, 123, 164
Okun, B., 39

Pareto, V., 38, 41
Perry, B. W., 114, 126
Peterson, F. M., 117
Phillips, C. E., 176
Pigou, A. C., 38
Plato, 131, 170, 186, 190, 191
Plessas, D., 70
Poletti, F., 170

Radzinowicz, L., 170
Reder, M., 167
Remy, M., 172
Ricardo, D., 27, 28
Richardson, R. W., 39
Ridker, R. G., 120, 123
Roberti, P., 40
Robinson, J. P., 95, 97, 98, 128
Rock, V. P., 168
Rousseas, S., 27

Sametz, A. W., 112, 116
Schumacher, E. F., 190
Schumpeter, J. A., 27
Scitovsky, T., 42, 116, 127, 166, 174, 175
Sheldon, E. B., 112
Shinohara, M., 114

Singer, S. F., 114, 126
Slutsky, E., 38
Smith, A., 5, 27, 28, 31, 36, 38
Smith, D., 169
Smith, V. K., 117
Solon, 135
Solow, R., 53, 118, 119, 125
Stobaugh, R., 118
Strumpel, B., 126
Syrquin, M., 39
Szalai, A., 166

Theodoracopoulos, I. N., 189
Thurow, L. C., 41
Tobin, J., 95, 113, 114, 115, 124, 125, 127, 128

Virgil, 170

Waldheim, K., 190
Weinberg, A. M., 121
Wilson, J., 169
Withey, S. B., 126, 142, 167

Xenophon, 170

Yergin, D., 118
Yu, E., 66, 67, 68, 123

Zeno of Citium, 189

BY THE SAME AUTHOR

IN ENGLISH, FRENCH AND GERMAN

Griechenland auf dem Wege zur Industrialisierung, Leipzig, 1926.

Wirtschaftsstruktur und Wirtschaftsbeziehungen Griechenlands, Leipzig, 1931.

L'étalon-or en théorie et en pratique, Paris, 1933.

Le question de l'or et le probléme monétaire, Paris, 1938.

La théorie économique traverse-t-elle une crise?, Paris, 1938.

La transformation du capitalisme, Paris, 1953.

Monetary Stability and Economic Development, Athens, 1958.

Economic Development and Technical Education, Athens, 1960.

The Problem of the International Monetary Liquidity, Athens, 1961.

Towards a Reinforced Gold Exchange Standard, Athens, 1961.

Economic Development and Private Enterprise, Athens, 1962.

International Monetary Order, Problems and Policies, Athens, 1962.

The Role of the Banks in a Developing Country, Athens, 1963.

The Multicurrency Standard and the International Monetary Fund, Athens, 1963.

Monetary Equilibrium and Economic Development, Princeton University Press, 1965.

Remodelling the International Monetary System, Athens, 1965.

Alternative Systems for International Monetary Reform, A Comparative Appraisal, Athens, 1965.

Current Monetary and Economic Developments in Greece, Athens, 1966.

International Labor Migration and Economic Development, Athens, 1966.

Monetary Planning, Athens, 1967.

The Gold Trap and the Dollar, Athens, 1968.

Speculocracy and the International Monetary System, Athens, 1969.

The International Money Mess, Athens, 1973.

From Anarchy to International Monetary Order, Athens, 1973.

The Energy Problem in Greece, Athens, 1975.

Recession and Reflation in the Greek Economy, Athens, 1975.

Developments and Prospects of the Greek Economy, Athens, 1975.

Guidelines for Industrial Development in Greece, Athens, 1976.

Greece in the European Community, Athens, 1976*.

International Monetary Vacillations, Athens, 1976*.

International Monetary Issues and Development Policies, New York
  University Press, 1977.

Inflation and the Monetary Target in Greece, Athens, 1978.

An International Loan Insurance Scheme, Athens, 1978.

The Positive Contribution of Greece to the European Community,
  Athens, 1978*.

The Dollar Crisis and Other Papers, Athens, 1979.

On the Issue of a Stable International Monetary Standard,
  Athens, 1981.

IN GREEK

The Quantity Theory of Money and Price Fluctuations, Athens,
  1927.

Foreign Exchange Theories, Athens, 1927.

Monetary and Foreign Exchange Phenomena in Greece 1910-1927,
  Athens, 1928.

Recent Developments in Theoretical Economics, Athens, 1929.

Monetary Stabilization, Athens, 1929.

The Tax Burden in Greece, Athens, 1930.

Bücher's Theory of Economic Stages and the World Economy, Thes-
  saloniki, 1930.

The Burden of Public Debt in Greece, Athens, 1931.

Monetary Studies, Athens, 1932.

Agricultural Policy, Athens, 1934.

Guidelines for our Economic Policy, Athens, 1936.

* Also in French translation.

Taxation, Saving and Investment, Athens, 1939.

Problems of Labor and Capital in Wartime, Athens, 1940.

Economics, Athens, 1942.

Creative Socialism, Athens, 1944.

Economic Fluctuations, Athens, 1944.

The Policy of the Bank of Greece, Athens, 1945.

The Factors of Social Welfare, Athens, 1946.

Economic Reconstruction and Viability, Athens, 1948.

The Monetary Problem and the Greek Economy, Athens, 1950.

Inflationary Pressures in the Greek Economy, Athens, 1951.

The Development Problem of the Economy, Athens, 1952.

Full Employment and Inflationary Pressures, Athens, 1954.

Lectures in Economic Theory, Athens, 1955.

Productive Investments and Guarantee Clauses in Bond Issues, Athens, 1957.

Regional Planning and Economic Development, Athens, 1961.

Money and the Economy — The Problem of Equilibrium, Athens, 1973.

The Orientation of Economic Policy, Athens, 1973.

The Contribution of Exports to Economic Development, Athens, 1976.

Social Welfare and Economic Organization, Athens, 1976.

Consumption, Investment and Monetary Equilibrium, Athens, 1977.

Economic and Monetary Problems in Greece, Athens, 1979.